WHAT COLOR IS YOUR PARACHUTE?

JOB-HUNTER'S WORKBOOK

FIFTH EDITION

A COMPANION TO THE BEST-SELLING
JOB-HUNTING BOOK IN THE WORLD

RICHARD N. BOLLES

TEN SPEED PRESS
California | New York

People often say that this or that person has not yet found himself.
But the self is not something one finds, it is something one creates.
—THOMAS SZASZ

Find what makes your heart sing and create your own music.
—MAC ANDERSON

When your heart speaks, take good notes.
—JUDITH CAMPBELL

Knowing yourself is the beginning of all wisdom.
—ARISTOTLE

Introduction

The Parachute Approach demands that you do an inventory of who you are and what you love to do, before you set out on your search for (meaningful) work.

Being out of work, or thinking about a new job or career, should speak to your heart. It should say something like this:

Use this opportunity. Make this not only a hunt for a job, but a hunt for a life. A deeper life, a victorious life, a life you're prouder of.

The world currently is filled with workers whose weeklong cry is, "When is the weekend going to be here?" And, then, "Thank God it's Friday!" Their work puts bread on the table but . . . they are bored out of their minds. They've never taken the time to think out what they uniquely can do, and what they uniquely have to offer to the world. The world doesn't need any more bored workers. Dream a little. Dream a lot.

How to Do a SELF-Inventory

You begin by stripping yourself (in your mind) of any past job-titles. When you ask yourself "Who am I?" you must drop the vocational answer that first springs to mind. Like: I'm an accountant, or I am a truck driver, or a lawyer, or a construction worker, or salesperson, or designer, or writer, or account executive. That kind of an answer locks you into the past. You must think instead: *"I am a person . . ."*

"I am a person who . . . has had these experiences."

"I am a person who . . . is skilled at doing this or that."

"I am a person who . . . knows a lot about this or that."

"I am a person who . . . is unusual in this way or that."

Yes, this is how a useful self-inventory begins. You are a person, not a job.

This self-inventory is a flower with *seven* petals (including the center). That's because there are seven sides to You, or seven ways of thinking about yourself, or seven ways of describing who you are—*using the language of the workplace.*

If you prefer a different metaphor, you are like a diamond, with seven facets to you, as we hold you up to the light.

1. *You and People.* You can describe *who you are* in terms of **the kinds of people** you most prefer to *work with or help*—age span, problems, handicaps, geographical location, etc.

2. *You and a Workplace.* Or you can describe *who you are* in terms of your favorite **workplace,** or **working conditions**—indoors/outdoors, small company/large company, windows/no windows, etc.—because they enable you to work at your top form, and greatest effectiveness.

3. *You and Skills.* Or you can describe *who you are* in terms of **what you can do,** and what your *favorite* functional/transferable skills are. For these are key to your being in top form, and at your greatest effectiveness.

4. *You and Your Purpose in Life.* Or you can describe *who you are* in terms of **your goals or sense of mission and purpose** for your life. Alternatively, or in addition, you can get even more particular and describe the goals or mission you want *the organization* to have, where you decide to work.

5. *You and the Knowledges You Already Have.* Or you can describe *who you are* in terms of **what you already know**—and what your *favorite* knowledges or interests are among all that stuff stored away in your head.

6. *You and Salary/Responsibility.* Or you can describe *who you are* in terms of **your preferred salary and level of responsibility**—working by yourself, or as a member of a team, or supervising others, or running the show—that you feel most fitted for, by experience, temperament, and appetite.

7. *You and Geography.* Or you can describe *who you are* in terms of **your preferred surroundings**—here or abroad, warm/cold, north/south, east/west, mountains/coast, urban/suburban/rural/rustic—where you'd be happiest, do your best work, and would most love to live, all year long, or part of the year, or vacation time, or sabbatical—either now, five years from now, or at retirement.

I Am a Person Who . . .

IS ALL THESE THINGS

You could choose just one, two, or three of these sides of yourself—let us say, "what you know," or "what you can do," or "your preferred salary"—as your guide to defining what kind of work you are looking for.

But what the Flower Diagram does is describe who you are in *all seven* ways, summarized on one page, in one graphic. After all, you are not just one of these things; you are *all* of these things. The Flower Diagram is a complete picture of *You*. All of you. In the language of the workplace.

And believe me, you want the complete picture. I'll tell you why. Let's say there is some job out there that matches just one petal, one side to yourself, one way of defining who you are: for example, let's say this job lets you use your favorite knowledges that you already have. But that's it.

That job doesn't let you use your favorite skills, nor does it have you working with the kinds of people you most want to, nor does it give you the surroundings where you can do your best work.

What would you call such a job? At the very least: *boring.* You would barely be able to wait for *Thank God it's Friday!* Some of us have already sung that song. A lot.

But now let us suppose you could instead find another kind of work that matches all seven sides of you. All seven petals. What would you call *that* work? Well, that's *your dream job.*

So, your complete Flower Diagram is a picture of who You most fully are. *And,* at the same time it is a picture of a job that would most completely match and fulfill all that you are. Where you would shine, because it uses the best of You.

Make it your goal to completely fill in your Flower. *And try to feel it as a joy rather than a duty.* Determine from the beginning that this is going to be fun. Because it sure can be. And should be.

The Flower

"That One Piece of Paper"

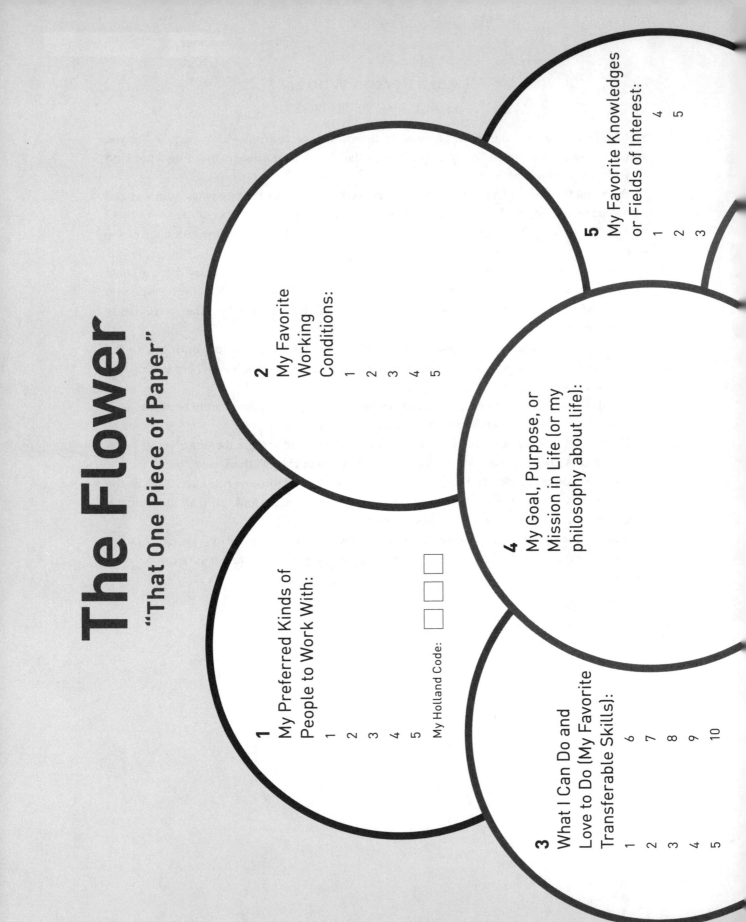

2
My Favorite
Working
Conditions:
1
2
3
4
5

1
My Preferred Kinds of
People to Work With:
1
2
3
4
5

My Holland Code:

3
What I Can Do and
Love to Do (My Favorite
Transferable Skills):
1   6
2   7
3   8
4   9
5   10

4
My Goal, Purpose, or
Mission in Life (or my
philosophy about life):

5
My Favorite Knowledges
or Fields of Interest:
1   4
2   5
3

7

My Preferred
Place(s) to Live:

1

2

3

My Preferred
Geographical
Factors:

1

2

3

4

5

6

Level of Responsibility I'd Like:

My Preferred Salary Range:

Other Rewards Hoped For:

PETAL 1

People

I Am a Person Who . . .

HAS THESE FAVORITE KINDS OF PEOPLE

My Preferred Kinds of People
to Work Beside or Serve

Goal in Filling Out This Petal: To avoid past bad experiences with people at work, since who (er, *whom*) you work with can either make the job delightful, or ruin your day, your week, your year.

What You Are Looking For: (1) A better picture in your mind of what kind of people surrounding you at work will enable you to operate at your highest and most effective level. (2) A better picture in your mind of what kind of people you would most like to serve or help: defined by age, problems, geography, and so forth.

Form of the Entries on Your Petal: They can be adjectives describing different kinds of people ("kind," "patient") or they can be types of people, as in the Holland Code or Myers-Briggs typologies (see pages 7–9 and 42, respectively).

Example of a Good Petal: Holland Code: IAS. (1) Kind, generous, understanding, fun, smart. (2) The unemployed, people struggling with their faith, worldwide, all ages.

Example of a Bad Petal: People in trouble, young, smart, in urban settings.

   Why Bad: Not much help. Too vague.

Petal 1, Worksheet #1

A HEXAGON: THE PARTY GAME EXERCISE

Every job or career has a **people-environment** that is characteristic of that career. Tell us what **career** or job interests you, and we can tell you, in general terms, what kind of people you would prefer to work with (from among six possibilities). Or start at the other end: tell us what kinds of people you prefer to work with—in terms of those same six factors—and we can tell you which careers will give you *that*.

It was Dr. John L. Holland who came up with this theory, and with a system for applying the theory to yourself. Surveying the whole workplace, he said there are basically six people-environments that jobs can give you. Let's tick them off (the quotes are John's definitions):

1. The **Realistic** People-Environment: Filled with people who prefer activities involving "the explicit, ordered, or systematic manipulation of objects, tools, machines, and animals." (*Realistic*, incidentally, refers to Plato's conception of "the real" as that which one can apprehend through the senses. "Knock on wood!")

   I summarize this as: **R** = *people who like nature, or plants, or animals, or athletics, or tools and machinery, or being outdoors.*

2. The **Investigative** People-Environment: Filled with people who prefer using their brain, specifically "the observation and symbolic, systematic, creative investigation of physical, biological, or cultural phenomena."

   I summarize this as: **I** = *people who are very curious, and like to investigate or analyze things, or people, or data.*

3. The **Artistic** People-Environment: Filled with people who prefer activities involving "ambiguous, free, unsystematized activities and competencies to create art forms or products."

   I summarize this as: **A** = *people who are very creative, artistic, imaginative, and innovative, and don't like time clocks.*[1]

4. The **Social** People-Environment: Filled with people who prefer activities involving "the manipulation of others to inform, train, develop, cure, or enlighten."

   I summarize this as: **S** = *people who are bent on trying to help, teach, or serve people.*

5. The **Enterprising** People-Environment: Filled with people who prefer activities involving "the manipulation of others to attain organizational or self-interest goals."

   I summarize this as: **E** = *people who like to start up projects or organizations, or sell things, or influence, or persuade, or lead people.*

6. The **Conventional** People-Environment: Filled with people who prefer activities involving "the explicit, ordered, systematic manipulation of data, such as keeping records,

---

1. Incidentally, there is a fascinating book about those whose primary code is "A." It's called *The Career Guide for Creative and Unconventional People* by Carol Eikleberry with Carrie Pinsky.

filing materials, reproducing materials, organizing written and numerical data according to a prescribed plan, operating business and data-processing machines." "Conventional," incidentally, refers to the "values" that people in this environment usually hold—representing the historic mainstream of our culture.

I summarize this as: **C** = *people who like detailed work, and like to complete tasks or projects.*

According to John's theory, every one of us *could become skilled in* all six, if we were given enough time. Instead, in the limited time we have from childhood to adulthood, we tend to develop preferences and survival skills in just **three** of these people-environments, and this is determined by who we grew up with, who we admired, and what time we gave to practicing expertise in these three people-environments, as we wended our way into adulthood. From among the six letters—RIASEC—you name your three preferred people-environments and this gives you what is called your "Holland Code," for example, SIA. Your question is, Which three?

I was friends with John for many years, and back in 1975 I invented a quick and easy way for you to find out your Code, based on John's Self-Directed Search (SDS). It turned out that it agrees with the results you would get from John's SDS, 92 percent of the time (this made John laugh). So if you want a more certain answer, you should take John's SDS ($9.95 at www.self-directed-search.com). But when you're in a hurry, this is close. And it's free. I call it "The Party Exercise." Here is how the exercise goes (*do it, please*):

On the opposite page is an aerial view of a room in which a party is taking place. At this party, people with the same interests have (for some reason) all gathered in the same corner of the room. And that's true for all six corners.

1. Which corner of the room would you instinctively be drawn to, as the group of people you would most enjoy being with for the longest time? (Leave aside any question of shyness, or whether you would have to actually talk to them; you could just listen.)

   Write the letter for that corner here: ☐

2. After fifteen minutes, everyone in the corner you chose leaves for another party across town, except you. Of the groups that still remain now, which corner or group would you be drawn to the most, as the people you would most enjoy being with for the longest time?

   Write the letter for that corner here: ☐

3. After fifteen minutes, this group too leaves for another party, except you. Of the corners, and groups, which remain now, which one would you most enjoy being with for the longest time?

   Write the letter for that corner here: ☐

The three letters you just chose are your Holland Code.[2]

Put that code here: ☐ ☐ ☐

Now, copy that code onto Petal #1, My Preferred Kinds of People to Work With, found on pages 4–5. So far, so good.

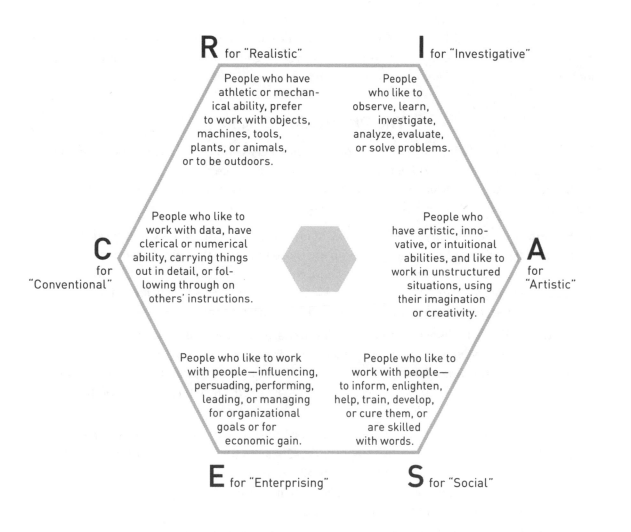

R for "Realistic"
People who have athletic or mechanical ability, prefer to work with objects, machines, tools, plants, or animals, or to be outdoors.

I for "Investigative"
People who like to observe, learn, investigate, analyze, evaluate, or solve problems.

C for "Conventional"
People who like to work with data, have clerical or numerical ability, carrying things out in detail, or following through on others' instructions.

A for "Artistic"
People who have artistic, innovative, or intuitional abilities, and like to work in unstructured situations, using their imagination or creativity.

E for "Enterprising"
People who like to work with people—influencing, persuading, performing, leading, or managing for organizational goals or for economic gain.

S for "Social"
People who like to work with people—to inform, enlighten, help, train, develop, or cure them, or are skilled with words.

---

2. Incidentally, John always encouraged people to write down somewhere all six versions (technically called *permutations*) of your code. Thus, if your code were, say, SIA, its permutations would be: SIA, SAI, IAS, ISA, ASI, AIS. This is especially useful if you are ever going to look up careers that correspond to your code. Put "Holland Codes for careers" into your favorite search engine, and you will find such sites as www.vista-cards.com/occupations.

   Further, he and I worked together on this application of his system to daydreams: list all the things you've ever dreamed of doing. Then, to the right of each, try to *guess*—guess!—at what you think the three-letter Holland Code would be for each. When done, look at each code and assign a value of 3 to any letter in the first position; assign a value of 2 to any letter in the second position; and assign a value of 1 to any letter in the third position (e.g., in the case of IAS, you'd give 3 points to "I," 2 points to "A," and 1 point to "S"). Do this for every code you've written down, then total up all the points for each letter. How many points did "R" get, how many points did "I" get, etc. Choose the top three with the most points, in order, when you're done, and you have the Holland Code of your daydreams. As John said to me, "This is the most reliable way of determining someone's code, but who would believe it, except you and me?"

Petal 1, Worksheet #2

A CHART: ENERGY DRAINERS VS. ENERGY CREATORS

Why do *the people you prefer* to be around matter at all—in the larger scheme of things? Because, the people we work with are either energy drainers or energy creators. They either drag us down and keep us from being our most effective, or they lift us up and help us to be at our best, and perform at our greatest effectiveness.

Here is an exercise to help you identify which is which, for you.

Start, of course, by filling in the first column in the chart on page 14, and then the second. This will bring you to the third column, and here you're gonna need some help. How do you look back at that stuff in the second column, and prioritize it? Well, you use:

The Prioritizing Grid

I give you my Prioritizing Grid. It asks you to decide between just two items at a time. The facing page shows what a ten-item Grid looks like, once it is completed.

(I originally had more than ten items as a result of that exercise, but by guess and by gosh I narrowed them down to my top ten, and then worked just with them.)

Section A. Here I put my list of ten items, in any order I choose. So, as you can see, the people I'd prefer not to have to work with are those who are: *bossy, never thank anyone, are messy in dress or office space, claim too much, are uncompassionate, never tell the truth, are always late, are totally undependable, feel superior to others,* or *never have any ideas.* The order in which I list these items here in Section A doesn't matter at all.

Section B. Here are displayed all the possible pairs among those ten. Each pair is in a little box, or rather, the *numbers* that represent each pair are in a little box. You ask each box a question. The framing of the question is crucial. The question you address to each box is: *"Between these two items, which is more important to me?"* Or, since this is a Grid of dislikes, *"Which of these two do I dislike more?"* (Think of choosing between two hypothetical jobs.)

Let's see how this works. We'll start with the first little box at the top. The box has the numbers 1 and 2 in it. (#1 stands for *bossy*, while #2 stands for *never thanks anyone*). So, the question is: *Which do you dislike more, #1 or #2?* You circle your preference in that box. I circled #1—as you can see—because I dislike being around bossy people at work more than I dislike being around ungrateful people.

You go on now to the second box (down diagonally to the southeast) which has in it the second pairing, in this case, the numbers 2 and 3. The question again: *Which do you dislike more?* I circled #3 in that box—as you can see—because I dislike being around messy people at work more than I dislike being around people who never thank anyone.

And so it goes, until you've circled one number in each little box in Section B.

PRIORITIZING GRID FOR 10 ITEMS OR LESS

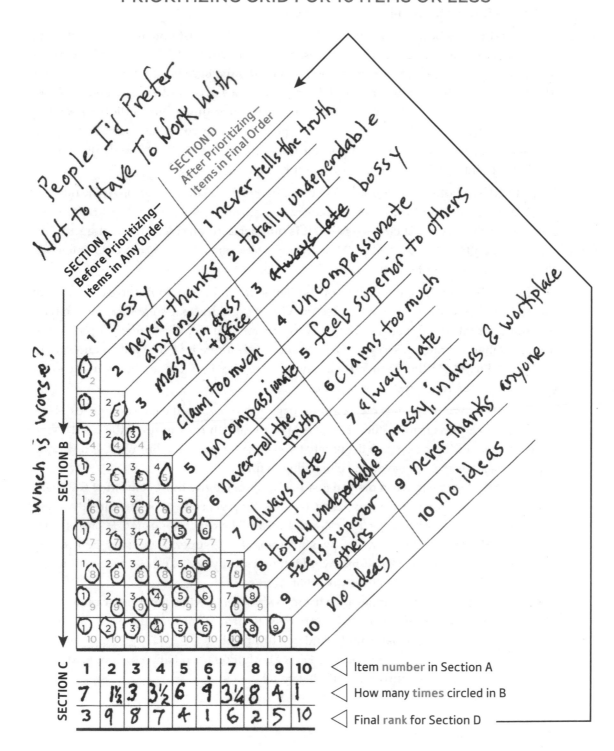

People I'd Prefer Not to Have To Work With

Which is worse?

SECTION A
Before Prioritizing—
Items in Any Order

SECTION D
After Prioritizing—
Items in Final Order

SECTION B

1 bossy
2 never thanks anyone
3 messy, in dress + office
4 claim too much
5 uncompassionate
6 never tell the truth
7 always late
8 totally undependable feels superior to others
9 no ideas

1 never tells the truth
2 totally undependable
3 always late
4 uncompassionate
5 feels superior to others
6 claims too much
7 always late
8 messy, in dress & workplace
9 never thanks anyone
10 no ideas

SECTION C	1	2	3	4	5	6	7	8	9	10	
	7	1½	3	3½	6	9	3½	8	4	1	◁ Item number in Section A
	3	9	8	7	4	1	6	2	5	10	◁ How many times circled in B
											◁ Final rank for Section D

◁ Item **number** in Section A
◁ How many **times** circled in B
◁ Final **rank** for Section D

Section C. Section C has three rows to it, at the bottom of the Grid, as you can see. The first row is just the ten numbers from Section A.

The second row is how many times each of those numbers just got circled in Section B. As you can see, item #1 got circled 7 times, item #2 got circled 1 time (as did item #10—a tie—so, to break the tie I look up in section B to find the little box that had both #2 and #10 in it, to see which I preferred at that time, and I see it was #2, so I give #2 an extra ½ point here, over #10). Item #3 I notice got circled three times, but so did item #4 and item #7—*a three-way tie!* How to break that tie? Well, here you'll just have to do some guessing. I guessed these were important to me in this order: #4, #7, and then #3. So, I added ½ point to #4 and ¼ point to #7; I left #3 as it was.

In the third and bottommost row of Section C, I put the ranking according to the number of circles in the second row. Item #6 got the most circles—9—so it is number 1 in ranking. Item #8 got the next most circles—8—so it is number 2 in ranking. And so it goes, until that whole bottom line is filled in. Now the only task remaining on this Grid is to copy the reorganized list onto Section D.

Section D. The aim here is to relist my ten items (from Section A) in the exact order of preference or priority, for me, using Section C as my guide. Item #6 got the most circles there, and it ranked number 1, so I copy the words for item #6 in the number 1 position in Section D. Item #8 ranked second, so I copy the words for item #8 into the second spot in Section D. Etc. Etc.[3] What I am left with, now, in Section D, is the ten items in the exact order of my preference and priority. *Nice!*

When you've completed your own Grid on page 13, go back to the chart on pages 14–15. Copy the first five items from Section D of the Grid into the third column of the chart. What you've got there, now, is a negative list of what you're trying to avoid. But what you want to end up with is a positive list of what you're trying to find.

So, look at the five negative items you just put up there, in the third column of the chart, and in the fourth column, write its opposite, or something near the opposite, directly opposite each item. By "opposite" I don't necessarily mean "the exact opposite." If one of your complaints in the third column was: "I was micromanaged, supervised every hour of my day," the opposite, in the fourth column, wouldn't necessarily be "No supervision." It might be "Limited supervision" or something like that. Your call.

Note that by first putting your negative list in exact order of what you **most want to avoid** (third column in the chart), your related positive list (fourth column) will have its factors in the exact order of what you **most want to find** in a future job.

Now copy the top five in column 4 onto Petal #1, My Preferred Kinds of People to Work With, on pages 4–5. And we are done (with that petal).

Time now to move on to another side of Who You Are.

---

3. Note that I made a mistake on line 3 in Section D. It never matters if you make a mistake. Just cross it out and jot down the correct information. It's okay not to be perfect.

PRIORITIZING GRID FOR 10 ITEMS OR LESS

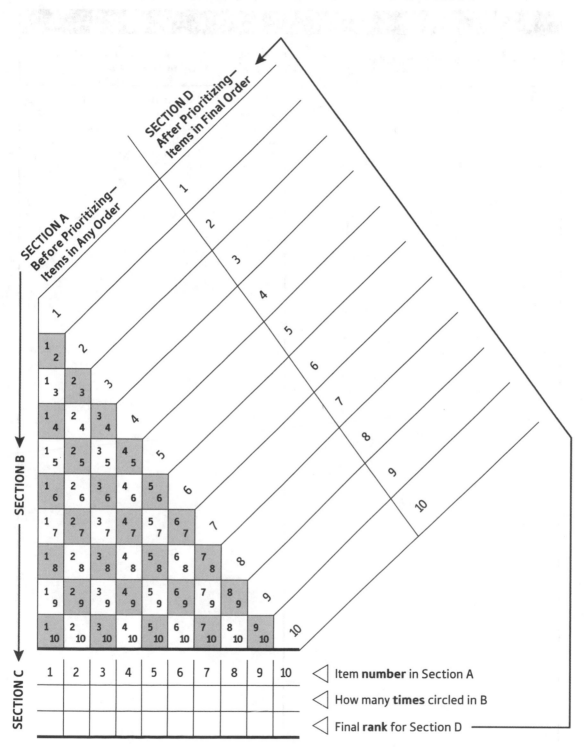

Item **number** in Section A

How many **times** circled in B

Final **rank** for Section D

MY FAVORITE PEOPLE

Column 1	Column 2
Places I Have Worked Thus Far in My Life	Kinds of People There Who Drove Me Nuts (from the first column)
	(No names, but describe what about them drove you nuts: e.g., bossy, always pestering me with their personal problems, always left early before the job was done, etc. List these in any order; it doesn't matter—at least in this column . . .)

MY FAVORITE PEOPLE

Column 3	Column 4
Kinds of People I'd Prefer Not to Have to Work With, in Order of Preference	Kinds of People I'd Most Like to Work With, in Order of Preference
(This is now a ranking of the items in the second column, in exact order of: which is worse? next? etc. Use the Prioritizing Grid on page 13 to do this.)	(The opposite of those qualities in the third column, in the same order)
1a.	1b.
2a.	2b.
3a.	3b.
4a.	4b.
5a.	5b.

PETAL 2

Working Conditions

I Am a Person Who . . .

HAS FAVORITE WORKING CONDITIONS

My Preferred Working Conditions

Goal in Filling Out This Petal: To state the working conditions and surroundings, that would make you happiest, and therefore enable you to do your most effective work.

What You Are Looking For: Avoiding past bad experiences.

Form of the Entries on Your Petal: Descriptors of physical surroundings.

Example of a Good Petal: A workspace with lots of windows, nice view of greenery, relatively quiet, decent lunch period, flexibility about clocking in and clocking out, lots of shops nearby.

Example of a Bad Petal: Understanding boss, good colleagues, fun clients, etc.

> **Why Bad:** These all belong on the petal called Preferred Kinds of People to Work With, not this one, which is just about the physical surroundings at your work, not the "people surroundings." Of course, since this is your Flower Diagram, you can put any info you like on any petal you like. It's just that if you want your thinking to be clear, it's useful to preserve the difference between "What is my preferred physical setting?" and "What kinds of people do I prefer to work with?" or "What clients/customers with what kinds of problems would I most like to help or serve?"

Your physical setting where you work can cheer you up or drag you down. It's important to know this before you weigh whether to take a particular job offer or not. The most useful way to do this has proved to be starting with working conditions that made you unhappy in the past, and then flip them over into positives, just as we did in the previous exercise.

Plants that grow beautifully at sea level often perish if they're taken ten thousand feet up the mountain. Likewise, we do our best work under certain conditions, but not under others. Thus, the question: "What are your favorite working conditions?" actually is a question about "Under what circumstances do you do your most effective work?"

Petal 2, Worksheet #1

A CHART: PHYSICAL ENVIRONMENTS
WHERE I WOULD THRIVE

As I just mentioned, the best way to approach this is by trying to remember all the things you *disliked* about *any* previous job, using the chart on pages 18–19 to list these. Column A may begin with such factors as "too noisy," "too much supervision," "no windows in my work-place," "having to be at work by 6 a.m.," etc.

As before, when you get to Column B, use a new ten-item Prioritizing Grid (on page 20).

This time, when you compare each two items, the frame you should put it in is, "If I were offered two jobs, and in the first job offer I would be rid of my distasteful working condition #1 but not #2, while in the second job offer I would be rid of my distasteful working condition #2, but not #1, which job offer would I take?"

After you've finished prioritizing, copy the first five items in Section D into Column B of your Distasteful Working Conditions chart, pages 18–19.

Once you have that list in Column B ranked—in terms of most distasteful down to least distasteful working conditions—turn to Column C in that chart and write *the opposite*, or something near *the opposite*, directly opposite each item in Column B.

Copy the five items in Column C onto Petal 2, the Favorite Working Conditions petal of your Flower Diagram, pages 4–5.

Okay, on to another side of Who You Are.

DISTASTEFUL WORKING CONDITIONS

Places I Have Worked Thus Far in My Life	Column A
	— Distasteful Working Conditions
	I Have Learned from the Past That My Effectiveness at Work Is Decreased When I Have to Work Under These Conditions

DISTASTEFUL WORKING CONDITIONS

Column B	Column C
− Distasteful Working Conditions Ranked	**+** The Keys to My Effectiveness at Work
Among the Factors or Qualities Listed in Column A, These Are the Ones I Dislike Absolutely the Most (in Order of Decreasing Dislike)	I Believe My Effectiveness Would Be at an Absolute Maximum If I Could Work Under These Conditions (The Opposite of the Qualities in Column B, in Order)
1a.	1b.
2a.	2b.
3a.	3b.
4a.	4b.
5a.	5b.

PRIORITIZING GRID FOR 10 ITEMS OR LESS

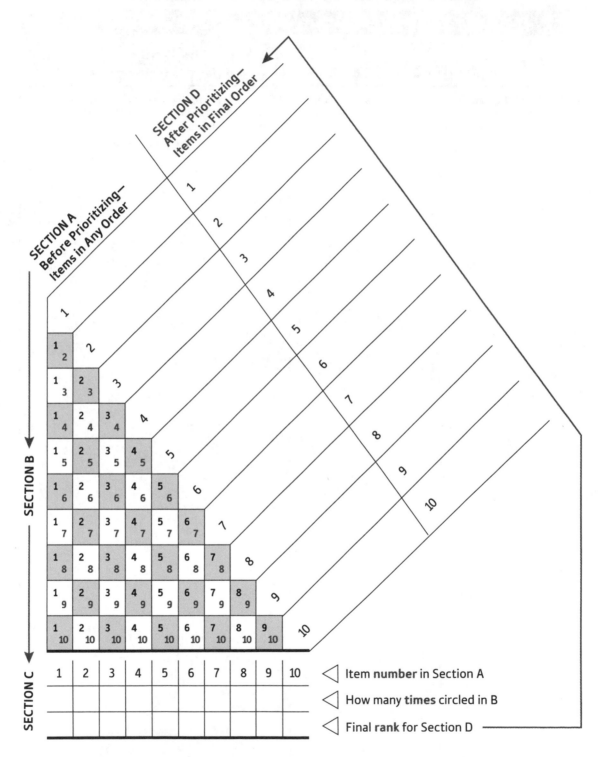

SECTION D
After Prioritizing—
Items in Final Order

SECTION A
Before Prioritizing—
Items in Any Order

SECTION B

SECTION C

1	2	3	4	5	6	7	8	9	10

◁ Item **number** in Section A

◁ How many **times** circled in B

◁ Final **rank** for Section D

PETAL 3

Transferable Skills

I Am a Person Who . . .

CAN DO THESE PARTICULAR THINGS

My Favorite Transferable Skills

Goal in Filling Out This Petal: To discover what your *favorite* functional skills are that can be transferred to any field of interest. They are things you probably were born knowing how to do, or at least you began with a natural gift and have honed and sharpened it since.

What You Are Looking For: Not just what you *can* do, but more particularly which of those you most *love* to use.

Form of the Entries on Your Petal: Verbs, usually in pure form (e.g., analyze), though they may sometimes be in gerund form (ending in -ing, e.g., analyzing).

Example of a Good Petal: (These stories show that I can) innovate, manipulate, analyze, classify, coach, negotiate; OR, to use the gerund form of these verbs, (these stories show that I am good at) innovating, manipulating, analyzing, classifying, coaching, negotiating.

Example of a Bad Petal: Adaptable, charismatic, reliable, perceptive, discreet, dynamic, persistent, versatile.

> **Why Bad:** These are all traits, or self-management skills; that is, they turn out to be the style with which you do your best, favorite, transferable skills. They are important, but they are not transferable skills. Incidentally, there is a new category floating around in the past ten years called "soft skills." These are really just another way of speaking about your skills with people, and/or your self-management skills, because examples typically are things like "a good work-ethic," "a positive attitude," "acting as a team player," "flexibility," "working well under pressure," and "ability to learn from criticism."

A Crash Course About Skills

"Skills" is one of the most misunderstood words in all the world of work. It begins with high school job-hunters: "I haven't really got any skills," they say. *Wrong!*

It continues with college students: "I've spent four years in college. I haven't had time to pick up any skills." *Wrong!*

And it lasts through the middle years, especially when a person is thinking of changing his or her career: "I'll have to go back to college, and get retrained, because otherwise I won't have any skills in my new field." Or: "Well, if I claim any skills, I'll have to start at a very entry kind of level." *Wrong!*

All of this confusion about the word "skills" stems from a total misunderstanding of what the word means. A misunderstanding that is shared, we might add, by altogether too many employers, human resources departments, and other so-called vocational experts.

By understanding the word, you will automatically put yourself way ahead of most job-hunters. And, especially if you are weighing a change of career, you can save yourself much waste of time on the adult folly called "I'll have to go back to school." I've said it before, and I'll say it again: *maybe* you need some further schooling, but very often it is possible to make a dramatic career-change without any retraining. It all depends. And you won't really *know* whether or not you need further schooling until you have finished all the exercises in this self-inventory.

So, let's begin again. Simple. Precise. Clear. What are skills? According to "the father" of the *Dictionary of Occupational Titles*, Sidney Fine, we all have three kinds of skills—abilities, talents, or whatever you want to call them.

SIDNEY FINE'S THREE KINDS OF SKILLS

Functional (Transferable) Skills	Special Knowledges	Self-Management Skills or Traits
WHAT YOU CAN DO and Love to Do with Data/ Statistics, People, or Things	WHAT YOU KNOW and Love to Use	HOW YOU CONDUCT YOURSELF Alone or with Others
USUALLY THESE ARE VERBS	USUALLY THESE ARE NOUNS	USUALLY THESE ARE ADJECTIVES OR ADVERBS
constructing	graphic design	adaptable
creating	physics	self-confident
researching	mathematics	cooperative
painting	warehouse	dependable
analyzing	procedures	enthusiastic
supervising	bookkeeping	disciplined
teaching	religion	flexible
illustrating	data analysis	innovative
organizing	auto repair	outgoing
counseling	Spanish	supportive
repairing	music	persistent
healing	principles of	resourceful
initiating	conference planning	tactful

We will deal with the first kind of skills, *Transferable Skills,* and the third, *Self-Management Skills,* in this section on Petal 3. We will save the second kind of skills, *Special Knowledges,* for Petal 5. So, let's begin with the *Functional or Transferable Skills.*

I recommend breaking down transferable skills into just three simple categories:

Are they skills you use with **information**, data, and the like,
or are they skills you use with **people**,
or are they skills you use with **things**?

Here are the most important truths to keep in mind:

1. **Your transferable (functional) skills are the most basic unit—the atoms—of whatever job or career you may choose.**

    Here is a famous diagram of them, invented by Sidney Fine.

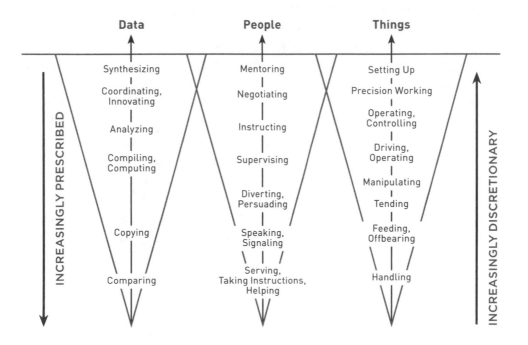

2. **You should always claim the highest skills you legitimately can, as demonstrated by your past performance.**

   As the diagram on the previous page makes clear, within each family there are *simple* skills, and there are higher, or *more complex* skills above them; these can be diagrammed as inverted pyramids, with the simpler skills at the bottom, and the more complex ones in order above them, for data, people, or things.

   Incidentally, as a general rule—to which there are exceptions—each *higher* skill requires you to be able to also do all those skills listed below it. So of course you can claim *those*, as well. But you want to especially emphasize the highest skill you legitimately can, on each pyramid, demonstrated by yourself at work or at play in the past.

3. **The higher your transferable skills, the more freedom you will have on the job.**

   As you can see from the side arrows in the diagram, simpler skills can be, and usually are, heavily *prescribed* (by the employer), so if you claim *only* the simpler skills, you will have to "*fit in*"—following the instructions of your supervisor, and doing exactly what you are told to do. The *higher* the skills you can legitimately claim, the more you will be given discretion to carve out the job the way you want to—so that it truly fits *you*.

4. **The higher your transferable skills, the less competition you will face for whatever job you are seeking, because jobs that use such skills will rarely be advertised through normal channels.**

   Not for you the way of classified ads, resumes, and agencies. No, if you can legitimately claim higher skills, you may then approach any organization that interests you, whether they have a known vacancy or not. Naturally, whatever places you visit—and particularly those that have not advertised any vacancy—you will find far fewer job-hunters whom you have to compete with.

   In fact, if the employers you visit happen to like you well enough, they may be willing to create for you a job that does not presently exist. *In which case, you will be competing with no one, since you will be the sole applicant for that newly created job.* As I mentioned earlier, while this doesn't happen all the time, it is astounding to me how many times it *does* happen. The *reason* it does is that the employers often have been *thinking* about creating a new job within their organization for quite some time—but with this and that, they just have never gotten around to *doing* it. Until you walked in.

   Then they decided they didn't want to let you get away, since *good employees are as hard to find as good employers*. And they suddenly remember that job they have been thinking about creating for many weeks or months now. So they dust off their *intention*, create the job on the spot, and offer it to you! And if that new job is not only what *they* need, but is exactly what *you* were looking for, then you have a dream job. Match-match. Win-win.

From our country's perspective, it is also interesting to note this: by this job-hunting initiative of yours, you have helped accelerate the creation of more jobs in your country, which is so much on everybody's mind here as we go deeper into the twenty-first century. How nice to help your country, as well as yourself!

5. **Don't confuse transferable skills with traits.**

Functional/transferable skills are often confused with traits, temperaments, or type. We often think that transferable skills are such things as: *has lots of energy, gives attention to details, gets along well with people, shows determination, works well under pressure, is sympathetic, intuitive, persistent, dynamic, dependable,* etc. These are not transferable skills, but *traits, self-management skills,* or *the style* with which you perform your transferable skills.

For example, let's assume that one of your traits is *"gives attention to details."* And let's suppose that one of your *transferable skills* is *"conducting research."* In that case, *"gives attention to details"* describes the manner or style with which you *conduct research.* More about this later.

Petal 3, Worksheet #1

A SKILLS CHART: ANALYZING SEVEN STORIES WHEN YOU WERE ENJOYING YOURSELF

Now that you know what transferable skills technically *are*, the problem that awaits you now is figuring out your own. If you are one of the few lucky people who already knows what your transferable skills are, blessed are you. Write them down, and put them in the order of preference, for you, on the Flower Diagram (pages 4–5).

If, however, you don't know what your skills are (and 95 percent of all workers *don't*), then you will need some help. Fortunately, there is an exercise to help. It involves the following steps.

1. Write One Story About Some Episode in Your Life (the First of Seven)

Yes, I know, I know. You can't do this exercise because you don't like to write. *Writers are a very rare breed.* That's what thousands of job-hunters have told me over the years. And for years I kind of believed them—until "texting" came along. Let's face it: we human beings are "a writing people," and we only need a topic we have a real passion for, or interest in—such as your life—for the writing genie to spring forth from within each of us, pen or keyboard in hand.

So, call the *Seven Stories from your life* that you're about to write your personal *offline blog*, if you prefer. But start writing. Please.

If you are finding it difficult to come up with seven stories, it may help you to know how others chose one or more of their stories:[1]

As I look back, I realize I chose a story that:

❑ Is somehow abnormal or inconsistent with the rest of my life

❑ Reveals my skills in a public way

❑ Is in a field (such as leisure, learning, etc.) far removed from my work

❑ I remembered through or because of its outcome

❑ Represented a challenge/gave me pride because it was something:

  • I previously could not do

  • My friends could not do

  • I was not supposed to be able to do

  • Only my father/mother could do, I thought

  • Only authorized/trained experts were supposed to be able to do

  • Somebody told me I could not do

  • My peers did not do/could not do

  • The best/brilliant/famous could or could not do

  • I did not have the right degree/training to do

  • People of the opposite sex usually do

❑ I would like to do again:

  • In a similar/different setting

  • With similar/different people

  • For free for a change/for money for a change

❑ Excited me because:

  • I never did it before

  • It was forbidden

  • I took a physical risk

  • I was taking a financial risk

  • No one had ever done it before

  • It demanded a long and persistent (physical/mental) effort

  • It made me even with someone

❑ I loved doing because:

  • I kind of like this sort of thing

  • The people involved were extremely nice

  • It did not cost me anything

❑ Will support/justify the professional goals I have already chosen

---

1. This list is the brainchild of Daniel Porot (© 1994 Daniel Porot).

Don't forget to look for skills that you use outside of work, such as those you use, or develop, playing video games (*strategic planning, navigating changing environments, active listening, communicating, collaborating, etc.*). Not only are these useful in various jobs and fields, but in and of themselves, video game skills can get you a scholarship to college—at least at Robert Morris University in Illinois, it can. If you absolutely can't think of any experiences you've had where you enjoyed yourself and accomplished something, then try this: describe the seven most enjoyable jobs that you've had, or seven roles you've had so far in your life, such as: wife, mother, cook, homemaker, volunteer in the community, citizen, dressmaker, student, etc. Tell us something you did or accomplished in each role.

Okay, the next step is actually writing. Here is one person's first story:

A number of years ago, I wanted to be able to take a summer trip with my wife and four children. I had a very limited budget, and could not afford to put my family up in motels. I decided to rig our station wagon as a camper.

First I went to the library to get some books on campers. I read those books. Next I designed a plan of what I had to build, so that I could outfit the inside of the station wagon, as well as topside. Then I went and purchased the necessary wood. On weekends, over a period of six weeks, I first constructed, in my driveway, the shell for the "second story" on my station wagon. Then I cut doors and windows, and placed a six-drawer bureau within that shell. I mounted it on top of the wagon, and pinioned it in place by driving two-by-fours under the station wagon's rack on top. I then outfitted the inside of the station wagon, back in the wheel-well, with a table and a bench on either side that I made.

The result was a complete homemade camper, which I put together when we were about to start our trip, and then disassembled after we got back home. When we went on our summer trip, we were able to be on the road for four weeks, yet stayed within our budget, since we didn't have to stay at motels. I estimate I saved $1,900 on motel bills during that summer's vacation.

As illustrated with this story, each story you write should have the following parts:

1. **Your goal: what you wanted to accomplish:** "I wanted to be able to take a summer trip with my wife and four children."

2. **Some kind of hurdle, obstacle, or constraint that you faced** (self-imposed or otherwise): "I had a very limited budget, and could not afford to put my family up in motels."

3. **A description of what you did, step by step** (how you set about ultimately achieving your goal, above, in spite of this hurdle or constraint): "I decided to rig our station wagon as a camper. First I went to the library to get some books on campers. I read those books. Next I designed a plan of what I had to build, so that I could outfit the inside of the station wagon, as well as topside. Then I went and purchased the necessary wood. On weekends, over a period of six weeks, I . . ." etc., etc.

4. **A description of the outcome or result:** "When we went on our summer trip, we were able to be on the road for four weeks, yet stayed within our budget, since we didn't have to stay at motels."

5. **Any measurable/quantifiable statement of that outcome,** that you can think of: "I estimate I saved $1,900 on motel bills during that summer's vacation."

Now write *your* story, using the sample as a guide.

Don't pick a story where you achieved something *big,* like: *"How I got my college degree over a period of ten years."* At least to begin with, write a story about some brief episode or task you accomplished, and you had fun!

Do not try to be *too* brief. This isn't Twitter.

2. Analyze Your First Story, Using the Skills Grid, to See What Transferable Skills You Used

Above the number 1 on page 30, write a brief title for your first story. Then work your way down the column below that number 1, asking yourself in each case: "Did I use this skill in this story?"

If the answer is "Yes," color in the little square for that skill, in that column, with a red pen or whatever.

Work your way through the entire Parachute Skills Grid that way, with your first story.

MY FIRST LIFE STORY

Your Goal (what you wanted to accomplish):

Some Kind of Obstacle (or Limit, Hurdle, or Restraint) You Had to Overcome Before It Could Be Accomplished:

What You Did Step by Step (it may help if you pretend you are telling this story to a whining four-year-old child who keeps asking, after each of your sentences, "An' then whadja do? An' then whadja do?"):

Description of the Result (what you accomplished):

Any Measure or Quantities to Prove Your Achievement:

THE PARACHUTE SKILLS GRID

Your Seven Stories

In the space to the left, write above each number, in turn, the name you give to each story. Begin with Story #1. Then go down the list of skills and mark the box if you used that skill in each story.

1	2	3	4	5	6	7	Skills with People; as my story shows, I can . . .
							Initiate, lead, be a pioneer
							Supervise, manage
							Follow through, get things done
							Motivate
							Persuade, sell, recruit
							Consult
							Advise
							Coordinate
							Negotiate, resolve conflicts
							Help people link up or connect
							Heal, cure
							Assess, evaluate, treat
							Convey warmth and empathy
							Interview, draw out
							Raise people's self-esteem
							Instruct
							Teach, tutor, or train (individuals, groups, animals)
							Speak
							Listen
							Counsel, guide, mentor
							Communicate well, in person
							Communicate well, in writing
							Divert, amuse, entertain, perform, act
							Play an instrument
							Interpret, speak, or read a foreign language
							Serve, care for, follow instructions faithfully
1	**2**	**3**	**4**	**5**	**6**	**7**	**Skills with Data, Ideas; as my story shows, I can . . .**
							Use my intuition
							Create, innovate, invent
							Design, use artistic abilities, be original

1	2	3	4	5	6	7	Skills with Data, Ideas; as my story shows, I can . . . (*continued*)
							Visualize, including in three dimensions
							Imagine
							Use my brain
							Synthesize, combine parts into a whole
							Systematize, prioritize
							Organize, classify
							Perceive patterns
							Analyze, break down into its parts
							Work with numbers, compute
							Remember people, or data, to unusual degree
							Develop, improve
							Solve problems
							Plan
							Program
							Research
							Examine, inspect, compare, see similarities and differences
							Pay attention to details
							Use acute senses (hearing, smell, taste, sight)
							Study, observe
							Compile, keep records, file, retrieve
							Copy

1	2	3	4	5	6	7	Skills with Things, or My Favorite Medium; as my story shows, I can . . .
							Control, expedite things
							Make, produce, manufacture
							Repair
							Finish, restore, preserve
							Construct
							Shape, model, sculpt
							Cut, carve, chisel
							Set up, assemble
							Handle, tend, feed
							Operate, drive
							Manipulate
							Use my body, hands, fingers, with unusual dexterity or strength

PETAL 3

3. Write Six Other Stories, and Analyze Them for Transferable Skills

Voilà! You are done with Story #1. However, "one swallow doth not a summer make," so the fact that you used certain skills in this first story doesn't tell you much. You have to keep writing stories—seven is the ideal, five is the minimum to be of any use—because what you are looking for is patterns—transferable skills that keep reappearing in story after story. They keep reappearing because they are your favorites (assuming you chose stories where you were *really* enjoying yourself).

So, write your Story #2, from any period in your life, analyze it using the skills grid, etc., etc. And keep this process up, until you have written, and analyzed, all your stories. A weekend should do it! In a weekend, you can inventory your *past* sufficiently so that you have a good picture of the *kind* of work you would love to be doing *in the future*. (You can, of course, stretch the inventory over a number of weeks, maybe doing an hour or two one night a week, if you prefer. It's up to you as to how fast you do it.)

MY SECOND LIFE STORY

Your Goal (what you wanted to accomplish):

Some Kind of Obstacle (or Limit, Hurdle, or Restraint) You Had to Overcome Before It Could Be Accomplished:

What You Did Step by Step (it may help if you pretend you are telling this story to a whining four-year-old child who keeps asking, after each of your sentences, "An' then whadja do? An' then whadja do?"):

Description of the Result (what you accomplished):

Any Measure or Quantities to Prove Your Achievement:

MY THIRD LIFE STORY

Your Goal (what you wanted to accomplish):

Some Kind of Obstacle (or Limit, Hurdle, or Restraint) You Had to Overcome Before It Could Be Accomplished:

What You Did Step by Step (it may help if you pretend you are telling this story to a whining four-year-old child who keeps asking, after each of your sentences, "An' then whadja do? An' then whadja do?"):

Description of the Result (what you accomplished):

Any Measure or Quantities to Prove Your Achievement:

MY FOURTH LIFE STORY

Your Goal (what you wanted to accomplish):

Some Kind of Obstacle (or Limit, Hurdle, or Restraint) You Had to Overcome Before It Could Be Accomplished:

What You Did Step by Step (it may help if you pretend you are telling this story to a whining four-year-old child who keeps asking, after each of your sentences, "An' then whadja do? An' then whadja do?"):

Description of the Result (what you accomplished):

Any Measure or Quantities to Prove Your Achievement:

MY FIFTH LIFE STORY

Your Goal (what you wanted to accomplish):

Some Kind of Obstacle (or Limit, Hurdle, or Restraint) You Had to Overcome Before It Could Be Accomplished:

What You Did Step by Step (it may help if you pretend you are telling this story to a whining four-year-old child who keeps asking, after each of your sentences, "An' then whadja do? An' then whadja do?"):

Description of the Result (what you accomplished):

Any Measure or Quantities to Prove Your Achievement:

MY SIXTH LIFE STORY

Your Goal (what you wanted to accomplish):

Some Kind of Obstacle (or Limit, Hurdle, or Restraint) You Had to Overcome Before It Could Be Accomplished:

What You Did Step by Step (it may help if you pretend you are telling this story to a whining four-year-old child who keeps asking, after each of your sentences, "An' then whadja do? An' then whadja do?"):

Description of the Result (what you accomplished):

Any Measure or Quantities to Prove Your Achievement:

MY SEVENTH LIFE STORY

Your Goal (what you wanted to accomplish):

Some Kind of Obstacle (or Limit, Hurdle, or Restraint) You Had to Overcome Before It Could Be Accomplished:

What You Did Step by Step (it may help if you pretend you are telling this story to a whining four-year-old child who keeps asking, after each of your sentences, "An' then whadja do? An' then whadja do?"):

Description of the Result (what you accomplished):

Any Measure or Quantities to Prove Your Achievement:

4. Patterns and Priorities

Okay, when you've finished this whole inventory, for all seven of your accomplishments/ achievements/jobs/roles or whatever, you want to look down your completed skills grid to discover any PATTERNS or PRIORITIES.

a. Patterns, because it isn't a matter of whether you used a skill once only, but rather whether you used it again and again. "Once" proves nothing; "again and again" is very convincing.

b. Priorities (that is, which skills are most important to you), because as we saw earlier, the job you eventually choose may not be able to use all of your skills. You need to know *what you are willing to trade off, and what you are not.* This requires that you know which skills, or family of skills, are most important to you.

So, after finishing your seven stories (or if you're in a hurry, at least five), look through that Skills Grid, and now guess which *might* be your top ten favorite skills. These should be your best guesses, and they should be about *your favorite* skills: not the ones you think the job market will like the best, but the ones *you* enjoy using the most.

At this point, now that you've guessed your top ten, you want to be able to list those ten *in exact order of priority.* Run your guesses through the Prioritizing Grid on page 40 and when you're done with that grid's Section D, copy the top ten onto your Favorite Transferable Skills petal on pages 4–5.

PRIORITIZING GRID FOR 10 ITEMS OR LESS

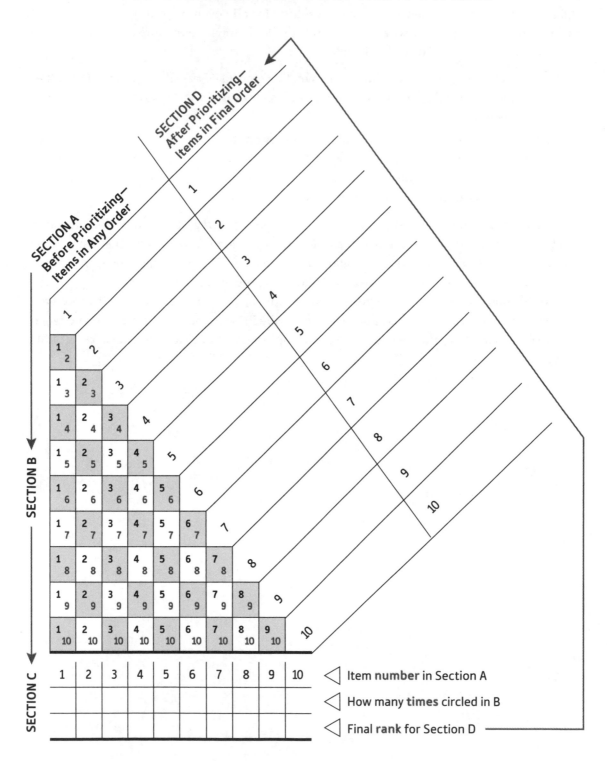

SECTION D
After Prioritizing—
Items in Final Order

SECTION A
Before Prioritizing—
Items in Any Order

SECTION B

SECTION C

1	2	3	4	5	6	7	8	9	10

◁ Item **number** in Section A

◁ How many **times** circled in B

◁ Final **rank** for Section D

5. Now Let's Turn to Your Self-Management Skills or Traits

A CHECKLIST OF YOUR STRONGEST TRAITS

I am very . . .

❑ Accurate

❑ Achievement-oriented

❑ Adaptable

❑ Adept

❑ Adept at having fun

❑ Adventuresome

❑ Alert

❑ Appreciative

❑ Assertive

❑ Astute

❑ Authoritative

❑ Calm

❑ Cautious

❑ Charismatic

❑ Competent

❑ Consistent

❑ Contagious in my enthusiasm

❑ Cooperative

❑ Courageous

❑ Creative

❑ Decisive

❑ Deliberate

❑ Dependable

❑ Diligent

❑ Diplomatic

❑ Discreet

❑ Driving

❑ Dynamic

❑ Effective

❑ Energetic

❑ Enthusiastic

❑ Exceptional

❑ Exhaustive

❑ Experienced

❑ Expert

❑ Extremely economical

❑ Firm

❑ Flexible

❑ Humanly oriented

❑ Impulsive

❑ Independent

❑ Innovative

❑ Knowledgeable

❑ Loyal

❑ Methodical

❑ Objective

❑ Open-minded

❑ Outgoing

❑ Outstanding

❑ Patient

❑ Penetrating

❑ Perceptive

❑ Persevering

❑ Persistent

❑ Pioneering

❑ Practical

❑ Professional

❑ Protective

❑ Punctual

❑ Quick/ work quickly

❑ Rational

❑ Realistic

❑ Reliable

❑ Resourceful

❑ Responsible

❑ Responsive

❑ Safeguarding

❑ Self-motivated

❑ Self-reliant

❑ Sensitive

❑ Sophisticated

❑ Strong

❑ Supportive

❑ Tactful

❑ Thorough

❑ Unique

❑ Unusual

❑ Versatile

❑ Vigorous

Now, let's go a little deeper.

In general, your self-management skills describe:

How you deal with time and promptness.

How you deal with people and emotions.

How you deal with authority and being told what to do at your job.

How you deal with supervision and being told how to do your job.

How you deal with impulse vs. self-discipline, within yourself.

How you deal with initiative vs. response, within yourself.

How you deal with crises or problems.

If you want to know what your traits or self-management skills are, popular tests such as the MBTI (the Myers-Briggs Type Indicator) measure that sort of thing.

If you have access to the Internet, there are clues, at least, about your traits or "type":

Working Out Your Myers-Briggs Type
www.teamtechnology.co.uk/tt/t-articl/mb-simpl.htm
An informative article about the Myers-Briggs

The 16 Personality Types
www.personalitypage.com/high-level.html
A helpful site about Myers types

What Is Your Myers-Briggs Personality Type?
www.personalitypathways.com/type_inventory.html
www.personalitypathways.com
Another article about personality types; also, there's a
Myers-Briggs applications page, with links to test resources

Myers-Briggs Foundation home page
www.myersbriggs.org
The official website of the foundation; lots of testing resources

Human Metrics Test (Jung Typology)
www.humanmetrics.com/cgi-win/JTypes2.asp
Free test, loosely based on the Myers-Briggs

Myers-Briggs Type Indicator Online
www.discoveryourpersonality.com/MBTI.html
On this site you can find the official Myers-Briggs test, $60

The Keirsey Temperament Sorter
http://keirsey.com
Free test, similar to the Myers-Briggs

You can use your self-management skills to flesh out each of your favorite transferable skills so that you are able to describe each of your talents or skills with more than just a one-word verb or gerund.

Let's take *organizing* as our example. You tell us proudly: "I'm good at organizing." That's a fine *start* at defining your skills, but unfortunately it doesn't yet tell us much. Organizing WHAT? People, as at a party? Nuts and bolts, as on a workbench? Or lots of information, as on a computer? These are three entirely different skills. The one word *organizing* doesn't tell us which one is yours.

So, please look at your favorite transferable skills, and ask yourself if you want to flesh out any of them with **an object**—some kind of Data/Information, or some kind of People, or some kind of Thing—plus **a self-management skill, or trait or style** (adverb or adjective).

Why is the trait important here? Well, "I'm good at organizing information painstakingly and logically" and "I'm good at organizing information in a flash, by intuition," are two entirely different skills. The difference between them is spelled out not in the verb, nor in the object, but in the adjectival or adverbial phrase there at the end. So, expand the definition of any of your ten favorite skills that you choose in the fashion I have just described.

When you are face to face with a person-who-has-the-power-to-hire-you, you want to be able to explain what makes you different from nineteen other people who can basically do the same thing that you can do. It is often the self-management skill, the trait, the adjective or adverb, that will save your life, during that explanation.

Now, on to the fourth side of Who You Are.

PETAL 4

Purpose
in Life

I Am a Person Who . . .

HAS A CERTAIN GOAL, PURPOSE, OR MISSION IN LIFE

My Purpose or Sense of Mission for My Life

Goal in Filling Out This Petal: To know the moral compass or spiritual values by which you want to guide your life. The most victorious life is one that is dedicated to some larger cause or mission.

What You Are Looking For: Some definition of the purpose and mission of your life. This may help you pick out the kinds of organizations or companies you'd like to work for, if you find ones that are serving the same mission as yours.

Form of the Entries on Your Petal: A description of what sphere of life you want to make better, with some attending details.

Example of a Good Petal: My purpose in life is to help the human spirit. I want there to be more faith, more compassion, more forgiveness, in families, because I have lived.

Example of a Bad Petal: More justice in the world.

    Why Bad: An admirable goal, but it is too vague. Doesn't give you any guidance as to what kind of justice to look for.

You need to dream about the broad outcome of your life, and not just this year's job search. What kind of footprint do you want to leave on this Earth, after your journey here is done? Figure that out, and you're well on your way to defining your life as having purpose and a mission. As John L. Holland famously said, "We need to look further down the road than just headlight range at night." The road is the road of Life.

Petal 4, Worksheet #1

DIAGRAM: THE NINE SPHERES OF PURPOSE OR MISSION

Generally speaking, purpose breaks down into nine spheres—corresponding to our nature. As you look these over on the diagram on page 47, the question is, which one appeals to *you* the most? Time for some hard thinking (ouch!). So, study the diagram *slowly*. Take time to ponder and think.

Now, let's look at these in more detail. Consider these as spheres, environments, or arenas in which you like to play.

1. **The Sphere of the Senses.** The question is: *When you have finished your life here on Earth, do you want there to be more beauty in the world, because you were here? If so, what kind of beauty entrances you? Is it art, music, flowers, photography, painting, staging, crafts, clothing, jewelry, or what?* If this is your main purpose in life, then write one paragraph about it.

2. **The Sphere of the Body.** The question is: *When you have finished your life here on Earth, do you want there to be more wholeness, fitness, or health in the world, more binding up of the body's wounds and strength, more feeding of the hungry and clothing of the poor, because you were here? What issue in particular?* If this is your main purpose in life, then write one paragraph about it.

3. **The Sphere of Our Possessions.** The question is: *Is your major concern the often false love of possessions in this world? When you have finished your life here on Earth, do you want there to be better stewardship of what we possess—as individuals, as a community, as a nation—in the world, because you were here? Do you want to see simplicity, quality (rather than quantity), and a broader emphasis on the word "enough," rather than on the words "more, more"? If so, in what areas of human life in particular?* If this is your main purpose in life, then write one paragraph about it.

4. **The Sphere of the Will or Conscience.** The question is: *When you have finished your life here on Earth, do you want there to be more morality, more justice, more righteousness, more honesty in the world, because you were here? In what areas of human life or history, in particular? And in what geographical area?* If this is your main purpose in life, then write one paragraph about it.

5. **The Sphere of the Heart.** The question is: *When you have finished your life here on Earth, do you want there to be more love and compassion in the world, because you were here? Love or compassion for whom? Or for what?* If this is your main purpose in life, then write one paragraph about it.

6. **The Sphere of Entertainment.** The question is: *When you have finished your life here on Earth, do you want there to be more lightening of people's loads, more giving them perspective, more helping them to forget their cares for a spell; do you want there to be more laughter in the world, and joy, because you were here? If so, what particular kind of entertainment do you want to contribute to the world?* If this is your main purpose in life, then write one paragraph about it.

7. **The Sphere of the Earth.** The question is: *Is the planet on which we stand your major concern? When you have finished your life here on Earth, do you want there to be better protection of this fragile planet, more exploration of the world or the universe—exploration, not exploitation—more dealing with its problems and its energy, because you were here? If so, which problems or challenges in particular draw your heart and soul?* If this is your main purpose in life, then write one paragraph about it.

8. **The Sphere of the Spirit.** The question is: *When you have finished your life here on Earth, do you want there to be more spirituality in the world, more faith, more compassion, more forgiveness, more love for God and the human family in all its diversity, because you were here? If so, with what ages, people, or with what parts of human life? If this is you, then your sense of purpose is pointing you toward the sphere of the spirit, or (if you prefer) the Kingdom of God.* If this is your main purpose in life, then write one paragraph about it.

9. **The Sphere of the Mind.** The question is: *When you have finished your life here on Earth, do you want there to be more knowledge, truth, or clarity in the world, because you were here? Knowledge, truth, or clarity concerning what in particular?* If this is your main purpose in life, then write one paragraph about it.

In sum, remember that all of these are worthwhile purposes and missions; all of these are necessary and needed in this world. The question is, which one in particular draws you to it *the most?* Which one do you most want to lend your brain, your energies, your skills, your gifts, and your life to serve while you are here on this Earth?[1]

When you are done, enter a summary paragraph of what you have decided your purpose or mission is on the Goal, Purpose, or Mission in Life petal on pages 4–5.

---

1. And by the way, if you want to have fun, if you have a computer, go to the Internet, type your sphere (*the Mind*, etc.) into the search line, and see if anything pops up that intrigues you.

THE PURPOSE FOR MY LIFE:
I WANT THERE TO BE MORE . . . (CHOOSE)

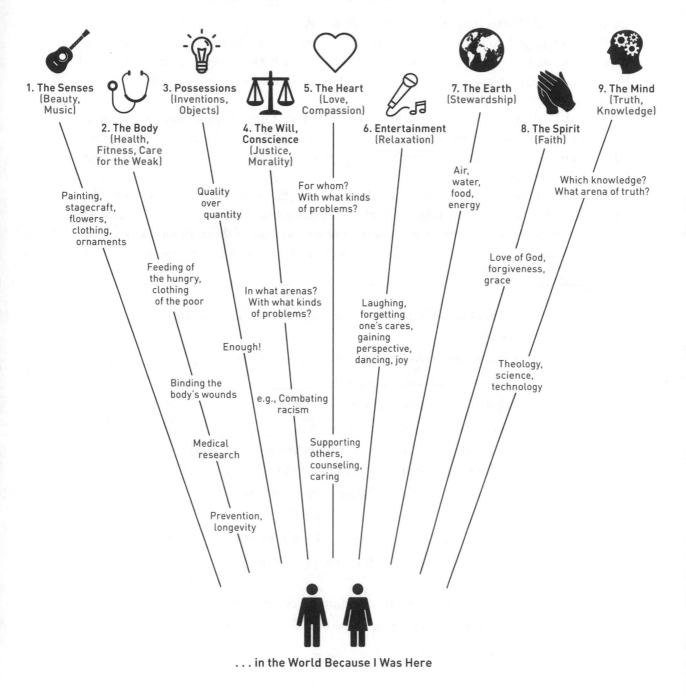

1. The Senses (Beauty, Music)
2. The Body (Health, Fitness, Care for the Weak)
3. Possessions (Inventions, Objects)
4. The Will, Conscience (Justice, Morality)
5. The Heart (Love, Compassion)
6. Entertainment (Relaxation)
7. The Earth (Stewardship)
8. The Spirit (Faith)
9. The Mind (Truth, Knowledge)

Painting, stagecraft, flowers, clothing, ornaments

Quality over quantity

For whom? With what kinds of problems?

Air, water, food, energy

Which knowledge? What arena of truth?

Feeding of the hungry, clothing of the poor

In what arenas? With what kinds of problems?

Love of God, forgiveness, grace

Enough!

Laughing, forgetting one's cares, gaining perspective, dancing, joy

Theology, science, technology

Binding the body's wounds

Medical research

e.g., Combating racism

Supporting others, counseling, caring

Prevention, longevity

. . . in the World Because I Was Here

Petal 4, Worksheet #2

ESSAY: YOUR PHILOSOPHY ABOUT LIFE

There are two challenges you may run into with this Petal.

First Challenge: You just come up empty on this exercise, despite hard thinking. No harm done. If you want an answer, just keep the question on the back burner of your mind; eventually, some insight is going to break through—tomorrow, next week, next month, or a year from now. Be patient with yourself.

Second Challenge: This subject doesn't grab you at all. Okay. Then instead of writing a statement of purpose or mission for your life, you can write instead a statement outlining what you think about *life*: why are we here, why are *you* here, and so on. This is often called "Your Philosophy of Life."

In writing a philosophy of life, it should be no more than two pages, single spaced, and can be less; it should address whichever of the elements listed below you think are most important; pick and choose. You do not have to write about all of them. In most cases, you will only need two or three sentences about each element you choose to comment on.

> **Beauty:** what kind of beauty stirs you; what the function of beauty is in the world
>
> **Behavior:** how you think we should behave in this world
>
> **Beliefs:** what your strongest beliefs are
>
> **Celebration:** how you like to play or celebrate in life
>
> **Choice:** what its nature and importance is
>
> **Community:** what your concept is about belonging to each other; what you think our responsibility is to each other
>
> **Compassion:** what you think about its importance and use
>
> **Confusion:** how you live with it and deal with it
>
> **Death:** what you think about it and what you think happens after it
>
> **Events:** what you think makes things happen; how you explain why they happen
>
> **Free will:** whether we are "predetermined" or have free will
>
> **Happiness:** what makes for the truest human happiness

Heroes and heroines: who yours are, and why

Humanity: what you think is important about being human; what you think is our function

Love: what you think about its nature and importance, along with all its related words: compassion, forgiveness, grace

Moral issues: which ones you believe are the most important for us to pay attention to, wrestle with, help solve

Paradox: what your attitude is toward its presence in life

Purpose: why we are here; what life is all about

Reality: what you think is its nature and components

Self: deciding whether physical self is the limit of your being; deciding what trust-in-self means

Spirituality: what its place is in human life, and how we should treat it

Stewardship: what we should do with God's gifts to us

Supreme Being: your concept of, and what you think holds the universe together

Truth: what you think about it; which truths are most important

Uniqueness: what you think makes each of us unique

Values: what you think about humanity; what you think about the world, prioritized as to what matters most (to you)

When you are done writing, put a summary paragraph on Petal 4, your Goal, Purpose, or Mission in Life, on pages 4–5.

Now, on to another side of Who You Are.

PETAL 5

Knowledges

I Am a Person Who . . .

ALREADY HAS (AND LOVES) THESE PARTICULAR KNOWLEDGES (OR INTERESTS)

My Favorite Knowledges, Interests, Subjects

Goal in Filling Out This Petal: To summarize all that you have stored in your brain. *Required:* From your past, subjects you already know a lot about, and enjoy talking about. *Optional:* For your future, what you would like to learn.

What You Are Looking For: Some guidance as to what field you would most enjoy working in.

Form of the Entries on Your Petal: Basically, they will all turn out to be nouns, but see below.

Example of a Good Petal: Graphic design, data analysis, mathematics, how to repair a car, video games, cooking, music, principles of mechanical engineering, how to run an organization, Chinese language, etc.

Example of a Bad Petal: Prompt, thorough, analyzing, persistent, communicating.

> **Why Bad:** Knowledges are always nouns. The words in the bad example above are not. In case you're curious, they are, in order: a trait (adjective), a trait (adjective), a transferable skill (verb), a trait (adjective), and a transferable skill (verb). All in all, that is one mixed bag! All are important, but you want only knowledges on this particular petal.

As mentioned in Petal 3, there are three things traditionally called skills: **knowledges**, as here; **functions**, *also known as transferable skills*; and **traits or self-management skills**. And as we saw there, a general rule throughout this inventory is that *knowledges are nouns; transferable skills are verbs;* and *traits are adjectives or adverbs.* If it helps knowing that, great; if not, *forget it!* Our overarching principle throughout this book is that if a generalization, a metaphor, or an example helps you, use it. But if it just confuses you, then ignore it!

On this Petal 5, you will eventually write your final results—your Favorite Knowledges/Fields of Interest, prioritized in the order of importance to you—on pages 4–5.

Petal 5, Worksheet #1

Q&A: TEN SHORTCUTS FOR IDENTIFYING YOUR FAVORITE KNOWLEDGES, SUBJECTS, FIELDS, OR INTERESTS (WHATEVER YOU WISH TO CALL THEM)

Jot down your answers to any or all of these ten shortcuts:[1]
1. What are your favorite hobbies or fields where you like to spend a lot of your time? (Computers? Gardening? Spanish? Law? Physics? Department stores? Hospitals? etc., etc.) Start a list.
2. What do you love to talk about? Ask yourself: if you were stuck on a desert island with a person who only had the capacity to speak on a few subjects, what would you pray those subjects were? If you were at a get-together, talking with someone who was covering two of your favorite subjects at once, which way would you hope the conversation would go? Toward which subject? If you could talk about something with some world expert, all day long, day after day, what would that subject or field of interest be? Add any ideas that these questions spark in you to your list.
3. What magazine articles do you love to read? I mean, what subjects? You get really interested when you see a magazine article that deals with . . . what subject? Add any ideas to your list.

---

1. I am indebted, again, to Daniel Porot of Geneva, Switzerland, for many of these suggestions.

4. What newspaper articles do you love to read? You get really interested when you see a newspaper special report that deals with . . . what subject? Add any ideas to your list.

5. If you're browsing in a bookstore, what sections of the bookstore do you tend to gravitate toward? What subjects there do you find really fascinating? Add any ideas to your list.

6. What sites on the Internet do you tend to gravitate toward? What subjects do these sites deal with? Do any of these really fascinate you? Add any ideas to your list.

7. If you watch TV, and it's a "game show," which categories would you pick? If it's an educational program, what kinds of subjects do you stop and watch? Add them to your list.

8. When you look at a catalog of courses that you could take in your town or city (or on the internet), which subjects really interest you? Add any ideas to your list.

9. If you could write a book, and it wasn't about your own life or somebody else's, what would be the subject of the book? Add it to your list.

10. There are moments, in most of our lives, when we are so engrossed in a task that we lose all track of time. (Someone has to remind us that it's time for supper, or whatever.) If this ever happens to you, what task, what subject, so absorbs your attention that you lose all track of time? Add it to your list.

Petal 5, Worksheet #2

CHART OF ALL THE THINGS YOU'VE LEARNED:
THE FISHER'S NET

The chart on page 55 is like **a commercial fisher's net,** where you want to cast it into the sea in order to capture the largest haul of fish possible, and only later do you pick out the best from your haul. But we start *big.*

How to fill out this chart? Well, that's your choice. You may want to fill this out at one sitting; or you may prefer to keep it in your pocket and jot down anything that occurs to you over a period of two or three weeks: every bright idea, every hunch, every remembered dream, every intuition that pops up. *This is an important petal—very important—as it may help you unearth a field or fields where you would really like to work. So it's worth spending some time on.*

Now here are some hints to help you fill in the first three parts of the chart.

PART 1. WHAT YOU KNOW FROM
YOUR PREVIOUS JOBS

If you've been out there in the world of work for some time, you've probably learned a lot of things that you now just take for granted. *"Of course I know* that!" But such knowledges may be important in and of themselves, or they may point you to something important down the line. So don't be afraid to really get detailed.

Examples: It can be things like: *bookkeeping, handling applications, credit collection of overdue accounts, hiring, international business, management, marketing, sales, merchandising, packaging, policy development, problem solving, troubleshooting, public speaking, recruiting, conference planning, systems analysis, the culture of other countries, other languages, government contract procedures,* and so on.

Think of each job you've ever held, and then for each job jot down any system or procedure that you learned there. For example: *"Worked in a warehouse: learned how to use a forklift and crane, inventory control, logistics automation software, warehouse management systems, teamwork principles, and how to supervise employees."* Or, *"Worked at a fast food place: learned how to prepare and serve food, how to wait on customers, how to make change, how to deal with complaints, how to train new employees, etc."*

PART 2. WHAT YOU KNOW OUTSIDE OF WORK

Jot down any bodies of knowledge that you picked up on your own just because the subject fascinated you, such as: *antiques, gardening, cooking, budgeting, decorating, photography, crafts, spirituality, sports, camping, travel, repairing things, flea markets, scrapbooking, sewing, art appreciation at museums, how to run or work in a volunteer organization,* and so on.

a. Also think of anything you learned in high school (or college) that you prize knowing today: *keyboarding? Chinese? accounting? geography?* Is this knowledge important to you? Figure that out later; for now, your goal is to just cast as wide a net as possible.

b. Think of anything you learned at training seminars, workshops, conferences, and so on, possibly in connection with a job you had at the time. Or something you decided to attend on your own. Jot it all down. Is this knowledge important to you? Figure that out later; for now, your goal is to just cast as wide a net as possible.

c. Think of anything you studied at home, via online courses, mobile apps, tape programs (likely played in your car while commuting), PBS television programs, etc. Is this knowledge important to you? Figure that out later; for now, your goal is to just cast as wide a net as possible. Jot it all down.

d. Think of anything you learned out there in the world, such as *how to assemble a flash mob, how to organize a protest, how to fund-raise for a particular cause, how to run a marathon, how to repair a toilet,* etc. Is this knowledge important to you? Figure that out later; for now, your goal is to just cast as wide a net as possible. Jot it all down, in the second section of the chart.

PART 3. WHAT FIELDS, CAREERS, OR INDUSTRIES
SOUND INTERESTING TO YOU

Broadly speaking, the workplace consists of the following six branches: *agriculture, manufacturing, information, technology, finance,* and *services.* Any ideas about which of these six is most attractive to you, right off the bat? If so, jot your answer down in the third section of the chart.

In order to drill down further into these six, your best bet is the government's O*Net OnLine (www.onetonline.org). O*Net OnLine has various lists of **career clusters** or **industries** or **job families**. On page 56 is a mashup of these. Please read over the list, and copy down any that you want to explore further (multiple choices preferred in order to have alternatives and therefore hope) in the third section of the chart.

THE FISHER'S NET

Notes About the Knowledges, Subjects, or Interests I've Picked Up Thus Far in My Life
1. What I Know from My Previous Jobs
2. What I Know About or Picked Up Outside of Work
3. What Fields, Careers, or Industries Sound Interesting to Me
4. Any Other Hunches, Bright Ideas, Great Ideas, etc. That Occur to Me

- ❏ Accommodation and Food Services
- ❏ Administrative and Support Services
- ❏ Agriculture, Food, and Natural Resources
- ❏ Architecture, Engineering, and Construction
- ❏ Arts, Audio/Video Technology, and Communications
- ❏ Business, Operations, Management, and Administration
- ❏ Community and Social Services
- ❏ Computer and Mathematical
- ❏ Design, Entertainment, Sports, and Media
- ❏ Distribution and Logistics
- ❏ Education, Training, and Library
- ❏ Entertainment and Recreation
- ❏ Farming, Forestry, Fishing, and Hunting
- ❏ Finance and Insurance
- ❏ Food Preparation and Serving
- ❏ Government and Public Administration
- ❏ Green Industries or Jobs
- ❏ Health Care, Health Science, and Social Assistance
- ❏ Hospitality and Tourism

- ❏ Human Services
- ❏ Information and Information Technology
- ❏ Law, Public Safety, Corrections, and Security
- ❏ Life, Physical, and Social Sciences
- ❏ Management of Companies and Enterprises
- ❏ Manufacturing
- ❏ Marketing, Sales, and Service
- ❏ Military Related
- ❏ Mining, Quarrying, and Oil and Gas Extraction
- ❏ Personal Care and Service
- ❏ Production
- ❏ Professional, Scientific, and Technical Services
- ❏ Protective Services
- ❏ Real Estate, Rental, and Leasing
- ❏ Religion, Faith, and Related
- ❏ Retail Trade, Sales, and Related
- ❏ Science, Technology, Engineering, and Mathematics
- ❏ Self-Employment
- ❏ Transportation, Warehousing, and Material Moving
- ❏ Utilities

Now, the nice thing about O*Net OnLine is that once you have chosen anything on the list above, the site has drop-down menus that allow you to go deeper into each *career cluster, industry,* or *job family* that you have checked off. It drills down to **career pathways**, and then drills down further to **individual occupations**, and then drills down still further to **tasks, tools, technologies, knowledges, skills, abilities, work activities, education, interests, work styles, work values, related occupations**, and **salary**.

The only limitation is that O*Net *only does this for about 900 occupations*. Its immediate predecessor, the D.O.T., had 12,741 occupations listed. So, O*Net does not offer a complete map of the job market by any means.

And even for those occupations that *are* listed in O*Net, remember: jobs, industries, and careers are *mortal*; they are born, they grow, they mature, and they flourish, then they decline and ultimately die. Sometimes it takes centuries, sometimes merely decades, sometimes even sooner than that. But eventually, most jobs, industries, and careers are mortal. It doesn't matter whether they were killed off by China or Mexico, or other supposed villains. They would have died anyway. Eventually.

We are mortal. So are jobs. Understand that truth and you will avoid a life of bitterness and blame. In today's world, you must *always* have a plan B up your sleeve.

Petal 5, Worksheet #3

PRIORITIZING YOUR KNOWLEDGES: FAVORITE SUBJECTS MATRIX

Okay, now you've completed worksheet #2. You've cast as wide a commercial fisher's net—so to speak—as possible, using Worksheet #1 and Worksheet #2 for this Petal. What now?

Well, it's time to pick the best of your haul, as we indicated earlier. Time to look it all over, and decide which knowledges, subjects, or interests are your favorites. Time for prioritizing. But we're going to use a different kind of prioritizing aid here: not our familiar Grid, but four boxes/compartments/"bins" along the axes of "Expertise" and "Enthusiasm." In other words, a matrix (page 58).

Then copy everything—*everything*—you have written down on Worksheet #1 (Ten Shortcuts) and Worksheet #2 (the Fisher's Net) and decide which of the four bins it belongs in, as you weigh your expertise (or lack of it) and your enthusiasm (or lack of it) with that particular subject or knowledge.

(You don't have to copy anything into bin #4 if you don't want to, except if you want bin #4 to stand there, filled with subjects and knowledges that you don't care about, as a cautionary tale. I'll state the obvious: any knowledge that you have neither any expertise in nor any enthusiasm for is a knowledge you will want to avoid at all costs in a future job, if it's up to you. And it is.)

Once you have finished copying every knowledge from Worksheets #1 and #2 into one of these bins, go back and study only what you put into bin #1: *High Expertise, High Enthusiasm.* Copy what you consider to be your top four or five favorites from that bin—*use a Prioritizing Grid if you need to*—and maybe, just maybe, one item from bin #2, and put them on Petal 5, found on pages 4–5.

Bueno! Your Favorite Subjects, Knowledges, Fields, Interests—whatever you want to call them—is done. Now you're ready to move on, to consider the sixth side of Who You Are.

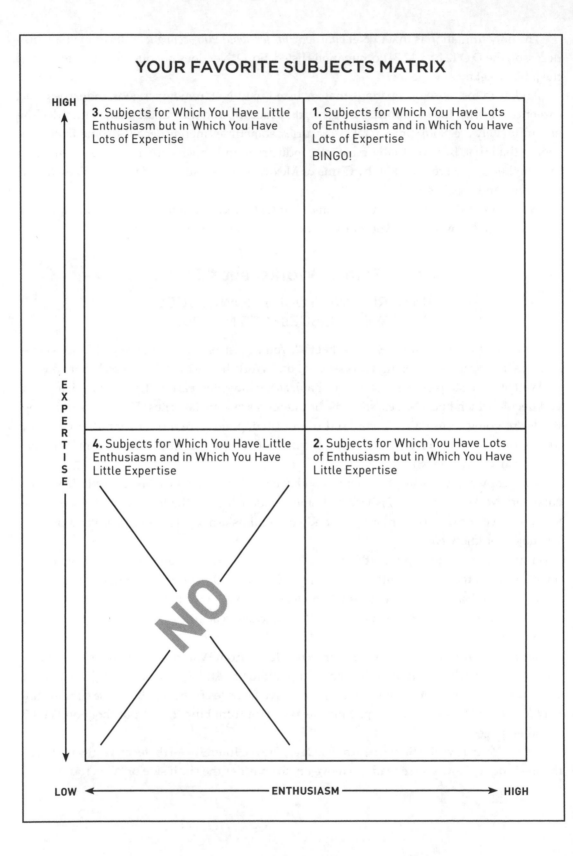

YOUR FAVORITE SUBJECTS MATRIX

HIGH

3. Subjects for Which You Have Little Enthusiasm but in Which You Have Lots of Expertise

1. Subjects for Which You Have Lots of Enthusiasm and in Which You Have Lots of Expertise
BINGO!

E X P E R T I S E

4. Subjects for Which You Have Little Enthusiasm and in Which You Have Little Expertise

2. Subjects for Which You Have Lots of Enthusiasm but in Which You Have Little Expertise

NO

LOW ⟵——————— ENTHUSIASM ———————➤ HIGH

PETAL 6

Salary

I Am a Person Who . . .

PREFERS A CERTAIN LEVEL OF RESPONSIBILITY AND SALARY

My Preferred Level of Responsibility and Salary

Goal in Filling Out This Petal: To gain a realistic picture of how much money you will need to earn, or want to earn, at whatever job you find.

What You Are Looking For: A range, because most employers are thinking in terms of a range, too. When you negotiate salary, as you will almost certainly have to, if the employer is of any significant size, you want the bottom of your range to be near the top of theirs.

Form of the Entries on Your Petal: Total dollars needed, weekly, monthly, or annually. Stated in thousands (symbol: K).

Example of a Good Petal: $75K to $85K

Example of a Bad Petal: $500K

    Why Bad: Well, it's not a range, which it needs to be; and it's too high unless you have a reason why such a high income is expected, and—more importantly—justified.

A Crash Course About Money

Money is important. Or else we're reduced to bartering for our food, clothing, and shelter. So, when we're out of work, unless we have huge amounts of money in our savings account or investments, we are inevitably thinking: "What am I going to do so that I have enough money to put food on the table, clothes on my back, and a roof over our heads for myself and for my family or partner (*if I have one*)?"

Happiness is important, too. So, we may find ourselves thinking: "How much do I really need to be earning for me to be truly happy with my life?"

Are these two worries—money and happiness—related? Can money buy happiness?

Partly, it turns out. Partly. A study, published in 2010, of the responses of 450,000 people in the United States to a daily survey found that the less money they made, the more unhappy they tended to be, day after day.[1] No surprise, there. And, obviously, the more money they made, measured in terms of percentage improvement, the happier they tended to be, *as measured by the frequency and intensity of moments of smiling, laughter, affection, and joy all day long, vs. moments of sadness, worry, and stress.*

So, money does buy happiness. *But only up to a point.* That point was found to be around $75,000 annual income. If people made more money than $75,000, it of course further improved their *satisfaction* with how their life was going, but it did not increase their happiness. Above $75,000, they started to report reduced ability to spend time with people they liked, to enjoy leisure, and to savor small pleasures. Happiness depends on things like that, and on other factors too: good health; a loving relationship; loving friends; and a feeling of competence, gaining mastery, respect, praise, or even love because we are really good at what we do.

So, this petal cannot be filled out all by itself. It is inextricably tied to the other petals— most particularly, to what you love to do and where you love to do it.

Still, salary is something you must think out ahead of time when you're contemplating your ideal job or career. Level goes hand in hand with salary, of course. So here are a couple of questions you should be asking yourself:

1. At what level would you like to work in your ideal job?

Level is a matter of how much responsibility you want in an organization:

❑ Boss or CEO (this may mean you'll have to form your own business)

❑ Manager or someone under the boss who carries out orders

❑ The head of a team

❑ A member of a team of equals

❑ One who works in tandem with one other partner

❑ One who works alone, as an employee, a consultant to an organization, or a one-person business

---

1. Daniel Kahneman and Angus Deaton, *Proceedings of the National Academy of Sciences*, Early Edition, September 6, 2010.

Think carefully about your answer, talk it over with your friends or family, then enter a two- or three-word summary of your answer (for now) on Petal 6, the Preferred Salary and Level of Responsibility, of your Flower Diagram, pages 4–5.

2. **What salary would you like to be aiming for?**

Here you have to think in terms of a range, not a single figure. One way to do this is to think of your minimum or maximum desired.

Minimum is what you would need to make if you were just barely "getting by." And incidentally, you do need to know this *before* you go in for a job interview with anyone (*or before you form your own business, and need to know how much profit you must make just to survive*). You can't survive on a negative income stream.

Maximum could be any astronomical figure you can think of, but it is more useful here to put down the salary you realistically think you could make, with your present competency and experience, were you working for a real, *but generous*, boss. (If this maximum figure is still depressingly low, then put down the salary you would like to be making five years from now.)

Petal 6, Worksheet #1

A BUDGET: KEEPING TRACK OF HOW MUCH YOU DO SPEND AND HOW MUCH YOU'D LIKE TO SPEND

Many job-hunters and career-changers want to begin by making up a budget of what they think they will need. On the next page you will find a simple guide to the categories you will need to think about. Figure out what you think you will need *monthly*, in each category. And if you see any categories missing, do not hesitate to add them.

Many do not want to start with a budget of how they *should* spend their money. They want to start by first keeping track of how, in actual fact, they *do* spend their money. You can just jot down notes at the end of each day. Lots of apps make this task much easier. For example, there is Spending Tracker, Pocket Expense, Goodbudget, and for all those who want to sync with their bank accounts, Mint.com.

The good news: all are simple, and all are free.

Once you figure out what you *do* spend, you'll be much better able to lay out a realistic budget of what you *want* to spend.

MONTHLY EXPENSES

Housing

Rent or mortgage payments . . . . $ _____

Electricity/gas . . . . $ _____

Water. . . . . $ _____

Phone/Internet . . . . $ _____

Garbage removal. . . . . $ _____

Cleaning, maintenance, repairs[2]. . . . . $ _____

Food

What you spend at the supermarket
and/or farmers' market, etc. . . . . $ _____

Eating out. . . . . $ _____

Clothing

Purchase of new or used clothing . . . . $ _____

Cleaning, dry cleaning, laundry . . . . $ _____

Automobile/transportation

Car payments . . . . $ _____

Gas (who knows?[3]) . . . . $ _____

Repairs . . . . $ _____

Public transportation (bus, train, plane) . . . . $ _____

Insurance

Car. . . . . $ _____

Medical or health care . . . . $ _____

House and personal possessions . . . . $ _____

Life . . . . $ _____

Medical expenses

Doctors' visits . . . . $ _____

Prescriptions . . . . $ _____

Fitness costs . . . . $ _____

---

2. If you have extra household expenses, such as a security system, be sure to include the quarterly (or whatever) expenses here, divided by three.

3. Your checkbook stubs and/or online banking records will tell you a lot of this stuff. But you may be vague about your cash or credit card expenditures. For example, you may not know how much you spend at the supermarket, or how much you spend on gas, etc. But there is a simple way to find out. Keep notes on your smartphone or iPad for two weeks (there are apps for that, such as DailyCost—$0.99). Jot down everything you pay cash (or use credit cards) for—on the spot, right after you pay it. At the end of those two weeks, you'll be able to take that record and make a realistic guess of what should be put down in these categories that now puzzle you. (Multiply the two-week figure by two, and you'll have the monthly figure.)

Support for other family members

Child-care costs (if you have children) . . . . $ _____

Child support (if you're paying that) . . . . $ _____

Support for your parents (if you're helping out) . . . . $ _____

Charity giving/tithe (to help others) . . . . $ _____

School/learning

Children's costs (if you have children in school) . . . . $ _____

Your learning costs (adult education, job-hunting classes, etc.) . . . $ _____

Pet care (if you have pets) . . . . $ _____

Bills and debts (usual monthly payments)

Credit cards . . . . $ _____

Local stores . . . . $ _____

Other obligations you pay off monthly . . . . $ _____

Taxes

Federal (next April's due, divided by twelve months) . . . . $ _____

State (likewise) . . . . $ _____

Local/property (next amount due, divided by twelve months) . . . $ _____

Tax help (if you ever use an accountant or

pay a friend to help you with taxes, etc.) . . . . $ _____

Savings . . . . $ _____

Retirement (Keogh, IRA, SEP, etc.) . . . . $ _____

Amusement/discretionary spending

Movies, Netflix, etc. . . . . $ _____

Other kinds of entertainment . . . . $ _____

Reading, newspapers, magazines, books . . . . $ _____

Gifts (birthdays, holidays, etc.) . . . . $ _____

Vacations . . . . $ _____

Total Amount You Need Each Month . . . . $ _____

In any event, by hook or by crook, once you have your monthly budget, it's time to do some math.

Multiply the total amount you need each month by 12, to get the yearly figure.

Divide the yearly figure by 2,000, and you will be reasonably near the *minimum* hourly wage that you need. Thus, if you need $3,333 per month, multiplied by 12 that's $40,000 a year, and then divided by 2,000, that's $20 an hour.

You will also want to put down the *maximum* salary you would like to make (dream, dream, dream). Once you are done, enter both salary figures—minimum and maximum—and any notes you want to add such as to justify the maximum (*you may also want to add any "nonmonetary" rewards you seek from the Optional Exercise below*) and add all of this onto Petal 6, the Preferred Salary Range and Level of Responsibility petal, found on pages 4–5.

Petal Six, Worksheet #2

AN OPTIONAL EXERCISE: OTHER REWARDS BESIDES MONEY

You may wish to put down other rewards, besides money, that you would hope for from your next job or career. These might be:

- ❏ Adventure
- ❏ Challenge
- ❏ Respect
- ❏ Influence
- ❏ Popularity
- ❏ Fame
- ❏ Power
- ❏ Intellectual stimulation from the other workers there

- ❏ A chance to be creative
- ❏ A chance to help others
- ❏ A chance to exercise leadership
- ❏ A chance to make decisions
- ❏ A chance to use your expertise
- ❏ A chance to bring others closer to God
- ❏ Other:

If you do check off things on this list, arrange your answers in order of importance to you, and then add them to the petal.

Now, on to the seventh side of Who You Are.

PETAL 7

Place

I Am a Person Who . . .
PREFERS CERTAIN PLACES TO LIVE

My Preferred Place(s) to Live

Goal in Filling Out This Petal: To define in what part of the country or the world you would most like to work and live, and be happiest, *if you ever have a choice.* Also to resolve a conflict (should it arise) between you and your partner as to where you want to live after you retire or make your next career move.

What You Are Looking For: Having a clearer picture about what you hope for in life, now or later. Now, if you're able to move and want to make a wise decision as to *where.* Later, if you're currently tied down to a particular place because "I need to be near my kids or my ailing parents," or whatever, in which case this becomes a planning for the future: retirement, or earlier. It's important to think about the future *now*, because an opportunity may come along when you least expect it, and you might pass right by it unless you've given it some thought and instantly recognize it.

Form of the Entries on Your Petal: You can stay general (*city, suburbs, rural, up in the mountains, on the coast,* or *overseas*) or you can get very specific if you're really ready to move, naming names and places—as this exercise will teach you to do.

Example of a Good Petal: First preference: Jackson, Wyoming; Second preference: Honolulu; Third preference: New York City.

Example of a Bad Petal: The West; a suburb; snow.

   Why Bad: Too broad. Doesn't really offer any help in making a decision. And it isn't prioritized, as a good petal must be.

Petal 7, Worksheet #1

A CHART: WHAT I LIKED OR DISLIKED ABOUT PLACES I HAVE LIVED

If you are doing this exercise with a partner, make a copy for them, so that each of you is working on a clean copy of your own, and can follow these instructions independently. Now, as to how you fill out the chart on pages 68–69:

Column 1. In *Column 1*, you should list all the places where you have ever lived. (If you are doing this exercise with a partner, they should make their own list on their own worksheet.)

Column 2. In *Column 2*, you should list all the factors you disliked (and still do) about each place. The negative factors do not have to be put exactly opposite the place in *Column 1*. The names in *Column 1* exist simply as pegs on which to hang your memory. If the same factors keep repeating, just put a check mark after the first listing of that factor every time it repeats. Keep going until you have listed all the factors you disliked or hated about each and every place you named in *Column 1*. Now, in effect, throw away *Column 1*; discard it from your thoughts. The negative factors were what you were after. *Column 1* has served its purpose. (*As you go, if you recall some things you liked about any place, list those factors at the bottom of the next column, Column 3.*)

Column 3. Look at *Column 2*, your list of negative factors, and in *Column 3* try to list each one's opposite (or near opposite). For example, "the sun never shone there" would, in *Column 3*, be turned into "mostly sunny, all year-round." It will not always be *the exact opposite*. For example, the negative factor "rains all the time" does not necessarily translate into the positive "sunny all the time." It might be something like "sunny at least 200 days a year." It's your call. Keep going, until every negative factor in *Column 2* is turned into its opposite, a positive factor, in *Column 3*. Don't forget to note any positive factors you listed at the bottom of *Column 3* when you were working on *Column 2*.

Column 4. In *Column 4*, now, list the positive factors in *Column 3*, in the order of most important (to you) down to least important (to you). For example, if you were looking at and trying to name a new town, city, or place where you could be happy and flourish, what is the first thing you would look for? Would it be good weather? Or lack of crime? Or good schools? Or access to cultural opportunities, such as music, art, museums, or whatever? Or would it be inexpensive housing? etc., etc. Rank all the factors in *Column 4*. Use the ten-item Prioritizing Grid on page 71 if you need to.

Show and tell. Once done, list on a blank sheet of paper those top ten factors, in order of importance to you, and show it to everyone you meet for the next ten days with the ultimate question: "Can you think of any place that has all ten of these factors, or at least the top five?" Jot down any and all of their suggestions on the back of the sheet. When the ten days are up, look at the back of that sheet and circle the three places that seem the most interesting to you. If there is only a partial overlap between your dream factors and the places your friends and acquaintances can come up with, *make sure the overlap is in the factors that count the most.*

Column 5. Now you have some names that you will want to find out more about, so that you can eventually figure out which would be your absolute favorite place to live, and your second, and your third, as backups. Enter those three places in *Column 5*, then copy them plus your top five geographical factors onto Petal 7, Preferred Place(s) to Live, on the Flower Diagram on pages 4–5.

Column 6. If you are doing this with a partner, skip *Column 5*. Instead, when you have finished your *Column 4*, look at your partner's *Column 4*, and copy it into *Column 6*. The numbering of *your* list in *Column 4* was 1, 2, 3, 4, etc. So, you need a different numbering system for your partner's list as you copy it into *Column 6*; let us say a, b, c, d, etc.

Column 7. Now, in *Column 7*, both of you can combine your *Column 4* with *Column 6* on your respective worksheets. Combine the two lists in this manner: first your partner's top favorite geographical factor ("a"), then *your* top favorite geographical factor ("1"), then your partner's second most important favorite geographical factor ("b"), then yours ("2"), etc., until you have twenty favorite geographical factors (*yours and your partner's*) listed, in order, in *Column 7*. Both of you are now working on the same list.

show and tell. (for two people). For now, don't work on all twenty; narrow it down to the top ten in column 7, and list these on a blank sheet of paper. Then both of you should show that list to everyone you meet, for the next ten days, with the same question as above: "Can you think of any place that has these ten factors, or at least the top five?" Jot down their suggestions on the back of the sheet. When the ten days are up, you and your partner should look at the back of your sheets and agree on which three places look the most interesting to the two of you. If there is only a partial overlap between your dream factors and the places your friends and acquaintances suggested, make sure the overlap is in the factors that matter the most to the two of you, i.e., those at the top of your list in *Column 7*.

Column 8. Now you have the names of places that you will want to find out more about, until you are sure which is the absolute favorite place to live for both of you, plus your second, and your third, as backups. Enter in *Column 8*.

Finally, both of you should put the names of those top three places, plus your top five geographical factors, onto Petal 7, the Preferred Place(s) to Live petal, on both of your Flower Diagrams, pages 4–5.

Note: Does all this seem like just too much work? Well, there are two shortcuts you *may* want to try. The first is a website called Teleport (teleport.org). Try it! See if it helps you at all. One reader said, "It showed me towns I'd never thought about."

Other alternative: have everyone in the house throw darts at a map (of the United States or wherever) that you've pinned to a dart board. One family did this after they couldn't agree on anything. See what place the most darts came near. (For them it came out: "Denver"! So, Denver it was!)

MY GEOGRAPHICAL PREFERENCES
Decision Making for Just You

Column 1	Column 2	Column 3
Names of Places I Have Lived	From the Past: Negatives	Translating the Negatives into Positives
		Factors I Liked and Still Like About Any Place

MY GEOGRAPHICAL PREFERENCES
Decision Making for Just You

Column 4	Column 5
Ranking of My Positives	Places That Fit These Criteria
1.	
2.	
3.	
4.	
5.	
6.	
7.	
8.	
9.	
10.	

OUR GEOGRAPHICAL PREFERENCES
Decision Making for You and a Partner

Column 6	Column 7	Column 8
Ranking of His/Her Preferences	Combining Our Two Lists (Columns 4 and 6)	Places That Fit These Criteria
a.	a.	
	1.	
b.	b.	
	2.	
c.	c.	
	3.	
d.	d.	
	4.	
e.	e.	
	5.	
f.	f.	
	6.	
g.	g.	
	7.	
h.	h.	
	8.	
i.	i.	
	9.	
j.	j.	
	10.	

PRIORITIZING GRID FOR 10 ITEMS OR LESS

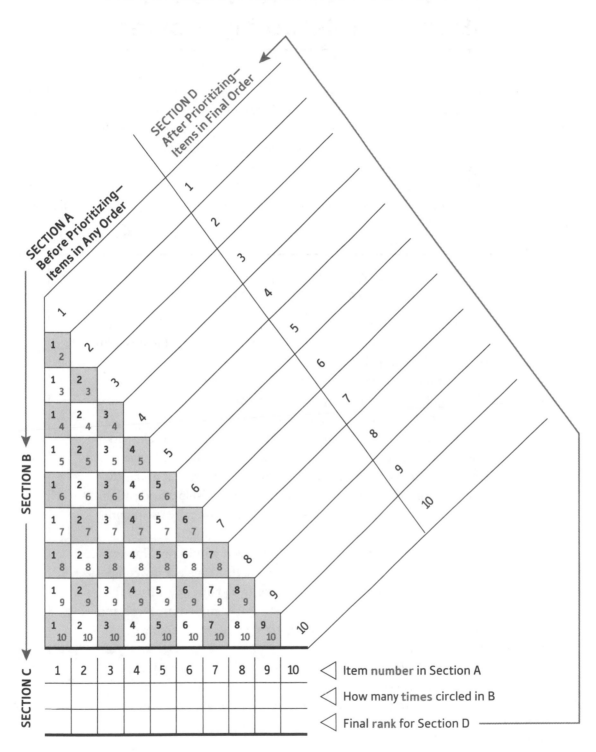

SECTION D
After Prioritizing—
Items in Final Order

SECTION A
Before Prioritizing—
Items in Any Order

SECTION B

SECTION C

◁ Item **number** in Section A

◁ How many **times** circled in B

◁ Final **rank** for Section D

I Am a Person Who . . .
Has Completed My Flower

Readers have asked to see an example of "That One Piece of Paper" all filled out. Rich W. Feller—a student of mine back in 1982, now a world-famous professor and past president of the National Career Development Association—filled out his flower, as you see, on the facing page. He said "That One Piece of Paper" has been his lifelong companion ever since, and his guiding star. (The petals then were slightly different.)

Rich Feller first put his personal "picture" together over thirty years ago. Here are his comments about its usefulness since, and how "That One Piece of Paper" helped him, how he's used it, and how it's changed.

WHAT THE PARACHUTE FLOWER HAS MEANT TO ME

More than anything I've gained from an academic life, my Flower has given me hope, direction, and a lens to satisfaction. Using it to assess my life direction during crisis, career moves, and stretch assignments, it helps me define and hold to personal commitments. In many ways it's my "guiding light." Data within my Flower became and remain the core of any success and satisfaction I have achieved.

After I first filled out my own Flower Diagram in a two-week workshop with Dick Bolles back in 1982, I decided to teach the Flower to others. My academic position has allowed me to do this, abundantly. Having now taught the Flower to thousands of counselors and career development and human resource specialists, I continually use it with clients, and in my own transitional retirement planning.

I'm overwhelmed with how little has changed within my Flower over the years. My Flower is the best of what I am. Its petals are my compass, and using my "favorite skills" is the mirror to a joyful day. I trust the wisdom within "That One Piece of Paper." It has guided my work and my life, ever since 1982, and it has helped my wife and I define our hopes for our son.

The process of filling out and acting on "That One Piece of Paper" taught me a lot. Specifically, it taught me **the importance of the following ten things, often running contrary to what my studies and doctoral work had taught me previously.**

(continued)

Example
(Rich Feller's Flower)

Favorite Values

1. Improve the human condition **2.** Promote interdependence and futuristic principles **3.** Maximize productive use of human/material resources **4.** Teach people to be self-directed/self-responsible **5.** Free people from self-defeating controls (thoughts, rules, barriers) **6.** Promote capitalistic principles **7.** Reduce exploitation **8.** Promote political participation **9.** Acknowledge those who give to the community **10.** Give away ideas

Favorite People-Environment

1. Strong social, perceptual skills **2.** Emotionally and physically healthy **3.** Enthusiastically include others **4.** Heterogeneous in interests and skills **5.** Social changers, innovators **6.** Politically, economically astute **7.** Confident enough to confront/cry and be foolish **8.** Sensitive to nontraditional issues **9.** I and R (see page 130) **10.** Nonmaterialistic

Favorite Interests

1. Large conference planning **2.** Regional geography & culture **3.** Traveling on $20/day **4.** Career planning seminars **5.** Counseling techniques/theories **6.** American policies **7.** Fundamentals of sports **8.** Fighting sexism **9.** NASCAR auto racing **10.** Interior design

Favorite Skills

1. Observational/learning skills • continually expose self to new experiences • perceptive in identifying and assessing potential of others **2.** Leadership skills • continually search for more responsibility • see a problem/act to solve it **3.** Instructing/interpreting/guiding • committed to learning as a lifelong process • create atmosphere of acceptance **4.** Serving/helping/human relations skills • shape atmosphere of particular place • relate well in dealing with public **5.** Detail/follow-through skills • handle great variety of tasks • resource broker **6.** Influencing/persuading skills • recruiting talent/leadership • inspiring trust **7.** Performing skills • getting up in front of a group (if I'm in control) • addressing small and large groups **8.** Intuitional/innovative skills • continually develop/generate new ideas **9.** Develop/plan/organize/execute • designing projects • utilizing skills of others **10.** Language/read/write • communicate effectively • can think quickly on my feet

Favorite Working Conditions

1. Receive clinical supervision **2.** Mentor relationship **3.** Excellent secretary **4.** Part of larger, highly respected organization with clear direction **5.** Near gourmet and health food specialty shops **6.** Heterogeneous colleagues (race, sex, age) **7.** Flexible dress code **8.** Merit system **9.** Can bike/bus/walk to work **10.** Private office with window

Geography

1. Close to major city **2.** Mild winters/low humidity **3.** Change in seasons **4.** Clean and green **5.** 100,000 people **6.** Nice shopping malls **7.** Wide range of athletic options **8.** Diverse economic base **9.** Ample local culture **10.** Sense of community (pride)

Salary and Level of Responsibility

1. Can determine 9/12 month contract **2.** Can determine own projects **3.** Considerable clout in organization's direction without administrative responsibilities **4.** Able to select colleagues **5.** 3 to 5 assistants **6.** $35K to $50K **7.** Serve on various important boards **8.** Can defer clerical and budget decisions and tasks **9.** Speak before large groups **10.** Can run for elected office

I learned from my Flower the importance of:

1. Chasing after passions, honoring strengths, and respecting skill identification

2. Challenging societal definitions of balance and success

3. Committing to something bigger than oneself

4. Living authentically and with joy

5. Being good at what matters to oneself and its relationship to opportunity

6. Finding pleasure in all that one does

7. Staying focused on well-being and life satisfaction

8. Personal clarity and responsibility for designing "possible selves"

9. Letting the world know, humbly but clearly, what we want

10. "Coaching" people amidst a world of abundance where individuals yearn for meaning and purpose more than they hunger for possessions, abject compliance with society's expectations, or simply fitting in

This technologically enhanced, global workplace we now face in the twenty-first century certainly challenges all we thought we knew about our life roles. Maintaining clarity, learning agility, and identifying development plans have become elevated to new and critical importance if we are to maintain choice. As a result, I've added the following four emphases to "Rich's Flower": Have, do, learn, and give. That is to say, I try to keep a running list (constantly updated) of ten things that I want to:

1. Have

2. Do

3. Learn

4. Give

Through the practice of answering the four questions listed above, I can measure change in my growth and development.

I feel so fortunate to have the opportunity to share with others how much I gained from the wisdom and hope embedded within "Rich's Flower."

> I humbly offer my resume and continuing work commitments on my website at *www.mychhs.colostate.edu/Rich.Feller.* I'd be honored to share my journey, and encourage others to nurture and shine light on their garden as well. I believe you'll find about 90 percent of the Flower's items influence our daily experience.
>
> **Rich Feller**
> **Professor of Counseling and Career Development**
> **University Distinguished Teaching Scholar**
> **Colorado State University**
> **Fort Collins, CO**

Okay, like Rich, you've now got your completed Flower: a picture of who you are, in all your glory. Also, a picture of a dream job that you can now go looking for.

You will now have one of two reactions as you look over your Flower.

A Light Bulb Goes On

For some of you there will be a big *Aha!* as you look at your Flower Diagram. A light bulb will go on, over your head, and you will say, "My goodness, I see *exactly* what sort of career this points me to." This happens particularly with intuitive people.

If you are one of those intuitive people, I say, "Good for you!" Just two gentle warnings, if I may:

Don't prematurely close out *other* possibilities.

And *don't* say to yourself: "Well, I see what it is that I would die to be able to do, but I *know* there is no job in the world like that, that *I* would be able to get." Dear friend, you don't know any such thing. You haven't done your research yet. Of course, it is always possible that when you've completed all that research, and conducted your search, you still may not be able to find *all* that you want—down to the last detail. But you'd be surprised at how much of your dream you may be able to find.

Other Possibility, You Look at Your Flower Diagram and . . . a Light Bulb *Doesn't* Go On

In contrast to what I just said, many of you will look at your completed Flower Diagram, and you won't have *a clue* as to what job or career it points to. Soooo, we need a "fallback" strategy.

First, write down on one piece of paper your top five favorite Transferable Skills and your top three favorite Knowledges from your Flower, and then ask at least five friends, family members, and professionals you know what job-titles and job-fields come to mind. Then, approach contacts in those fields for Informational Interviews. During Informational Interviewing, you want to talk to people who are actually doing the work you think you'd love to do. Why? In effect, you are mentally *trying on jobs* to see if they fit you.

Once you discover places you'd like to work for, do some preliminary research on them before you approach them for an interview.

And remember, always send a thank-you note to anyone who helps you along the way.

Need More Help?

This should get you started toward finding your dream job, with the Flower as your guide. For more information on job-hunting, I invite you to consult with the book for which this workbook is a companion: *What Color Is Your Parachute? A Practical Manual for Job-Hunters and Career-Changers*, by yours truly.

Don't just drop your Flower at this point. Be persistent, be thorough, and don't give up just because your Flower doesn't immediately point you toward the next step. Keep showing your Flower to anyone and everyone, and ask what suggestions they can make. This is your life you're working on, your *Life*. Make it glorious.

About the Author

DICK BOLLES—more formally known as Richard Nelson Bolles—led the career development field for more than four decades. He was featured in *Time*, the *New York Times*, *Businessweek*, *Fortune*, *Money*, *Fast Company*, the *Economist*, and *Publishers Weekly*, and appeared on the *Today* show, CNN, CBS, ABC, PBS, and other popular media. Bolles keynoted hundreds of conferences, including the American Society for Training & Development and the National Career Development Association. A member of Mensa, the Society for Human Resource Management, and the National Resume Writers Association, he was considered "the most recognized job-hunting authority on the planet" (*San Francisco Chronicle*) and "America's top career expert" (*AARP*).

Time magazine chose *What Color Is Your Parachute?* as one of the hundred best nonfiction books written since 1923. The Library of Congress chose it as one of twenty-five books down through history that have shaped people's lives. It appeared on the *New York Times* best-seller list for more than five years. The book has sold ten million copies, to date, and has been translated into twenty languages and used in twenty-six countries.

Bolles was trained in chemical engineering at Massachusetts Institute of Technology, and earned a bachelor's degree cum laude in physics from Harvard University, a master's in sacred theology from General Theological (Episcopal) Seminary in New York City, and three honorary doctorates. He passed away in 2017 at age ninety after a lifetime of service to job-hunters across the world.

WHAT COLOR IS YOUR PARACHUTE?

A Practical Manual for Job-Hunters and Career-Changers

10,000,000 COPIES SOLD

$19.99 paper (Canada: $25.99)

6 x 9 inches, 352 pages

ISBN 978-0-399-58168-7

Available from TEN SPEED PRESS
wherever books are sold.
www.tenspeed.com

Previous editions of this work were published in 1998, 2005, 2010,
and 2012 by Ten Speed Press, Berkeley, CA.
Some text in this workbook has been adapted from chapter 5 of
What Color Is Your Parachute? 2019.

The drawings on pages 23 and 32 are by Steven M. Johnson, author of *What the
World Needs Now*. Meeting icon on pages 2 and 6 by Björn Andersson, Workspace
icon on pages 2 and 16 by Universal Icons, Help icon on pages 2 and 21 by Luis
Prado, Dawn icon (slightly altered) on pages 2 and 44 by Stephen Plaster, Brain
icon on pages 2, 47, and 50 by Wes Breazell, Personal finance icon on pages 2 and
59 by Gregor Crešnar, Hand icon on page 22 by Chameleon Design, Stopwatch
icon on page 22 by Nick Holroyd, Guitar icon on page 47 by Hum, Stethoscope
icon on page 47 by Ralf Schmitzer, Light bulb icon on page 47 by AB, Scale icon
on page 47 by Edward Boatman, Heart icon on page 47 by Maria Maldonado,
Singing icon on page 47 by Creative Stall, Earth icon on page 47 by João Proença,
Praying icon on page 47 by Cristiano Zoucas, Rest room icon on page 47 by lipi,
from thenounproject.com.

ISBN 978-0-399-58189-2

Printed in the United States of America

10 9 8 7 6 5 4 3 2

Fifth Edition